Transformational Daydreaming

How to Talk with Your Subconscious Mind and Daydream Your Way to a Better Life

Timothy A. Storlie, PhD

Copyright © 2017 Timothy A. Storlie
All rights reserved.
ISBN-10: 1475222424
ISBN-13: 9781475222425

DEDICATION

For my wife Debra Belshee-Storlie—an extraordinary woman, lifelong daydreamer, and gifted psychologist. Her editorial assistance, creative content contributions, and unwavering belief in me, in us, and in this book, played a huge role in bringing this dream to completion.

CONTENTS

	Acknowledgments	i
1	Transformational Daydreaming	1
2	Befriend the Subconscious Mind	17
3	Accelerated Learning	31
4	All About Daydreaming	51
5	Step 1 – Go to Your Safe Place	65
6	Step 2 – Relax and Entered Altered State	77
7	Step 3 – Contemplate to Communicate	89
8	Steps 4 – 7	109
9	The Complete 7-Step Process	123
10	37 Applications and 22 Tools	139
11	Psychic and Spiritual Daydreaming	151
	Master List of All Chapter Main Points	165
	About the Author	197

ACKNOWLEDGMENTS

For Dr. Stanley Krippner—world-class scholar and mentor—whose collective body of work is truly inspirational and who was instrumental in the development of my interests in night dreaming, and daydreaming.

CHAPTER 1

TRANSFORMATIONAL DAYDREAMING — PRACTICAL HOPE

This is a workbook about hope—the practical hope of creating a better life. How? By learning to communicate with your subconscious mind using the tools of contemplation and daydreaming.

Hope is the optimistic belief that people and circumstances can improve—that life can get better. What about you? What are some of the things you hope for? Improved health? Professional success? Better relationships? More money? A more fulfilling life? I hope for a better life—for me, for you, for everyone. That's one reason I wrote this book.

Hope is a helpful, necessary, important *force*. But—when change is wanted, needed, or required—is the force of hope alone enough? I don't believe so. Truth is, if you hope to *feel* different—if you hope that life will somehow *be* different—then you must *do* something different.

Whether you hope that things will go your way, go away, or come your way, by itself, hope is not enough to make it happen. Why?

Because, in between hoping and having, some *doing* is required. This *doing* requires some type of form (or methods) for the force to work through. The formula is simple,

Hoping + Doing = Having

To make things better, hope has to be practical. It has to have a form (or methods) for nudging a desired possibility toward a greater probability—for transforming the theoretical into the actual. This book presents an original nudging method—the 7-step form of transformational daydreaming.

> "The first step to better times is to imagine them." — Chinese fortune cookie.

The quote above, offers sage advice. To this advice, I would add, your first step to better times—or to better health, a better relationship, better finances, a better job, a better sex life, or to a better anything—is to first hope, contemplate, and daydream about it. This book will show you exactly how to do this.

Accelerated Learning—The Key Question

Frequent repetition of important information is a basic tool of accelerated learning. Repetition is used throughout this book to help quicken your learning, deepen your understanding, and increase your retention.

Here are some other suggestions for accelerating your learning, increasing comprehension and retention, and getting the most from this book. Begin each chapter by first turning to the *List of Main Points* at end of the chapter so you can *preview* what you will read.

After completing your preview, then carefully *read* the chapter and complete each exercise.

As you study each chapter, read with the *key question* in mind. This will help focus and organize your thoughts. By keeping the key question in mind, you'll not only rapidly learn more, but you'll retain more of what you do learn.

The overarching key question for *Part I* of this book is,

> *"How can I learn to communicate with my subconscious mind and daydream my way to a better life?"*

This book was written to help answer this important question. Finally, *review* what you learned by re-reading the *List of Main Points*. This process, faithfully followed, will help maximize your learning experience. Also, for your easy preview, review, and reference, you'll find a *Master List of the Collective Main Points* from each chapter located at the back of this book. More detailed suggestions on how to get the most from your learning efforts are offered in chapter 3.

Introduction to 7-Step Transformational Daydreaming Process

Transformational daydreaming is a special way of using the power of your imagination to develop a working relationship between the conscious mind and the subconscious mind so you can create a better life.

If you study the information in all 7 steps, understand what you read, sincerely involve yourself with the content, and complete all the suggested practices, you'll learn to use what I believe is one of the most powerful self-help techniques available—how to communicate and receive advice from your subconscious mind.

In this workbook, your subconscious mind is also referred to as the *super intelligence within* or sometimes as the *wise inner Elder*. Other authors have called it the *Inner* Advisor or the *High Self*.

Chapter two provides detailed information about the subconscious mind. To help you accurately frame your developing view, here's a preview of the 7-step communication process you'll learn.

1. Go to your Safe Place—an imagined or actual place where you feel safe, relaxed, and comfortable.
2. Relax and enter an altered state of awareness.
3. Contemplate to communicate your concerns to your subconscious mind. *This is how you ask for help*.
4. Receive a daydream from your subconscious mind. Your subconscious mind responds to your request using the symbolic language of daydreams. These daydreams offer insight, advice, and guidance regarding your concerns. *This is how you receive help*.
5. Return to normal, wakeful awareness. Reorient yourself and return to alert, normal, wakeful awareness.
6. Exit your Safe Place.
7. Document, analyze, and interpret your daydream. Transform insight into action. Document and analyze the advice received from the subconscious mind via your daydream.

Once you've learned and practiced this method, you can begin to explore the numerous creative uses to help accelerate learning and performance; experience more fun, fantasy, and entertainment; improve communication, relationships and sexual intimacy; achieve personal fulfillment; and/or experience greater personal, professional, and spiritual growth and development (see chapter 10 for a description of more than 37 areas of your life you can improve with transformational daydreaming).

The Seeds of Transformational Daydreaming

The seeds of transformational daydreaming were planted when I was a young school boy. I often sat at my small wooden desk staring impatiently out the window, wondering if the dismissal bell would ever ring—absorbed by the mental movies playing on the inner screen of my mind—I would daydream of the adventures awaiting me when I arrived back home.

My daydreams often depicted a group of friends and me making a bee-line for the woods and then running down the path that led to the creek. After all these years, I can still remember how real these imagined adventures felt. For example: I could smell the creek water and feel the slippery, moss-covered log under my feet—the bridge we used to cross the creek. I could feel the excited anticipation of what was on the other side, our secret rope swing—the key to our next great Tarzan adventure.

Unfortunately, my daydream escapades were often rudely interrupted by a stern warning issued by a teacher who believed daydreaming was an enormous waste of time. But she was wrong. In fact, many now consider daydreaming to be a hidden wellspring of learning and creativity masquerading as idleness (Lahey, 2013).

Contrary to my teacher's old-fashioned opinion, many contemporary psychologists now view daydreaming as normal, healthy, and helpful (Gayle Group, 2001). And, it is the "helpful" and "hopeful" benefits of daydreaming that are the central focus of this book.

Who Daydreams?

You might be wondering who daydreams? The short answer is, probably everyone, and probably more often than you think (Fries, 2009; Singer, 2009). Some research suggests people spend one-half or more of their waking life in a daydream (Klinger, 1990; Lehrer, 2012). As far as anyone knows, even dogs daydream.

Applications and Benefits of Transformational Daydreaming

After you complete this program, you can expect to begin to discover the many exciting and beneficial applications of daydreaming. In the chapters to follow, you'll learn:

- The power, creativity, and wisdom of your subconscious mind.
- How to "talk" with your subconscious mind using contemplation and daydreaming.
- At least 37 ways you can use daydreaming for personal, professional, business, creative, artistic, psychic, spiritual, and transpersonal growth.
- How to increase your physical, emotional, and psychological well-being.
- How to enrich communication, relationships, and sexual pleasure.
- To better manage anxiety, depression, fear, grief, stress, bad habits and destructive patterns.
- How to feel more relaxed, balanced, centered, focused, hopeful, and peaceful.
- Methods for practicing and improving any behavior, skill, or sport.
- The countdown method for developing deep relaxation.
- Quick methods for entering an altered state of awareness where learning is often easier, deeper, and more permanent.
- The practical nuts and bolts of contemplation and daydreaming.
- Advanced techniques to increase the power and effectiveness of your work.
- Secrets to accelerated learning. And more!!!

The Documented Power of Mental Imagery

The use of positive mental imagery and visualization to promote and improve your health has been around for more than three decades (Fries, 2009). Research has consistently demonstrated the benefits of using mental imagery for helping to reduce pain, promote health and wellness, accelerate learning, and enhance performance in the arts and in sports health (Sheikh, 1989).

Sophisticated brain scans, near-infrared spectroscopy measurements, and other instruments show that during mental imaging, many of the same parts of the brain are activated that would be if what you are imaging was physically occurring. When a specific skill is visualized, a measurable increase of blood flow to that area of the body was observed (Siddle, 2008).

Contemporary psychiatrists, psychologists, counselors, social workers, and hypnotherapists, often use imagery-based techniques when conducting therapy. This is especially true when helping others to reduce or better manage symptoms of anxiety, depression, grief, fears, phobias, for smoking cessation, weight loss, for relaxation training, stress management, and improving relationships and parenting.

Imagery is the dominant language of the right brain and of the unconscious (Rossman, 2000). Dr. Bressler—co-founder and co-director of the academy for guided imagery—describes imagery as one of the two higher-order languages of the human nervous system. Sheikh (1989) argues that imagery is the language of the unconscious. Dozens of studies have demonstrated that mental imagery can affect nearly every major system of your body. For example: imagery has been used to help with immune system problems, stroke rehabilitation, and with the pre-preparation and post-recovery processes associated with various medical and dental procedures.

Within the field of sports psychology, the use of mental imagery is widely accepted as an effective method for improving your athletic performance. Convincing physiological evidence exists that supports the effectiveness of tactical imagery. Siddle (2008) wrote that "when athletes were attached to biofeedback monitors and imaged a skill, very small electrical signals could be detected in muscles of the same body parts involved when the skill is actually executed" (p.173). Imagery is also frequently used in educational settings to accelerate and improve the effectiveness of the learning process and facilitate acquisition of academic skills.

Transformational daydreaming can also be used to help cultivate your artistic and creative skills. Daydreaming can benefit various activities such as acting, dancing, speaking, writing, song writing, poetry, sculpting, painting, or improving musical performance. You can use daydreaming to test-drive career options—mentally trying them out to discover what you think and how you feel—without committing yourself (Singer, 1975).

Whatever activities you daydream about, the process of daydreaming mobilizes many of the same areas of the brain that would be used if you were physically engaged in these activities (Klinger, 1990). For example, daydreaming playing the piano helps to create or reinforce neuronal pathways in the brain associated with that activity. This underscores the effectiveness of using daydreams to practice and rehearse various activities before physically doing them.

Transformational Daydreaming and Business Success

Within the field of business, there are many applications for daydreaming. Innovation, marketing, strategic planning, and creative product development are all areas that can benefit from transformational daydreaming. Many of today's innovation-related success stories come from companies that pay employees to daydream on the job—companies such as Google, 3M, WL Gore and Associates (Fries, 2009).

Today's businesses (high-tech or product design companies), often depend upon the constant generation of new concepts. By encouraging key employees to daydream when they're on the job (and on the clock) and to come up with fresh, marketable ideas, these companies are much more likely to benefit from any novel or breakthrough concepts that come from these employees. For example, cloud computing was developed by day dreamers at work (Fries, 2009).

Many key executives (and employees) also use daydreaming to help prepare for important meetings, presentations, and interviews. The bottom line is, that in a rapidly changing, highly competitive business climate, daydreaming could just be the competitive edge needed.

Erotic Daydreaming

At one time or another, nearly everyone daydreams about sex or desired relationships. Some more than others. But either way, daydreams of love and sex are some of the most common daydreams people have (Klinger, 1990).

Daydreaming about sexual intimacy with your lover or partner—

especially when apart—is very common. It's also common to explore, experiment, and try out new and novel sexual experiences first in your daydreams. Many people find that erotic daydreaming can enhance their sexual and intimate experiences and help cultivate an exciting, and deeply satisfying sex life (Fries, 2009).

Transpersonal, Psychic, and Paranormal Daydreaming

In addition to improving physical, emotional, and mental skills and abilities, some people find transformational daydreaming is an effective tool for developing various psychic, mystical, and transpersonal skills. This is discussed at length in chapter 11. A small sample of possibilities includes:

- Developing ESP, telepathy, and remote viewing.
- Experiencing out-of-body travel.
- Communicating with animals.
- Visiting with the deceased.
- Traveling through time.
- Improving mindfulness, meditation and other spiritual practices.
- Expanding awareness.

In the inner world of your daydreams, you can experience new adventures, relive old ones, and rehearse the future without risk (Glausiusz, 2014). It's up to you.

> *"If you can dream it, you can do it."*
> *– Walt Disney*

In the next chapter, you will be introduced to the subconscious mind—the super-intelligence that dwells within you.

List of Main Points for Preview and Review

- ✓ This is a workbook about hope—the practical hope of creating a better life. How? By learning to communicate with your subconscious mind using the tools of contemplation and daydreaming.

- ✓ Hope is the optimistic belief that people and circumstances can improve—that life can get better. The force of hope is helpful. But—when change is wanted, needed, or required—is it enough? I don't believe so. Truth is, if you hope to *feel* different—if you hope that life will somehow *be* different—then, you must *do* something different. In between hoping and having, some *doing* is required.

- ✓ To make things better, hope has to be practical. It has to have a form (or methods) for nudging a desired possibility toward a greater probability—for transforming the theoretical into the actual.

- ✓ This *doing* requires some type of form for the force to work through. The formula is simple—hoping + doing = having.

- ✓ This book presents a practical, 7-step program on how to communicate and receive advice from the subconscious mind. Using contemplation and daydreaming, you can seek advice on how to experience greater personal, professional, and spiritual growth and development.

- ✓ Frequent repetition of important information is a basic tool of accelerated learning. Repetition is used throughout this book to help quicken your learning, deepen your understanding, and increase your retention.

- ✓ To accelerate your learning, increase comprehension and retention, and get the most from this book, begin each chapter by first turning to the end of the chapter so you can *preview* the list of main points. After completing your preview, then carefully *read* the chapter and complete each exercise. As you study each chapter, read with the key question in mind. Finally, *review* what you learned by re-reading the list of main points. Also, for your easy preview, review, and reference, you'll find a master list of the collective main points from each chapter located at the back of this book.

✓ Research has consistently demonstrated the benefits of using mental imagery for helping to reduce pain, promote health and wellness, accelerate learning, and enhance performance in the arts and in sports.

✓ The process of daydreaming mobilizes many of the same areas of the brain that would be used if you were physically engaged in these activities. This underscores the effectiveness of using daydreams to practice and rehearse various activities before physically doing them.

✓ For your easy preview, review, and reference, you'll find a master list of the main points from each chapter at the back of this book.

References

Bristow, W. (2004). *The art of the daydream.* London, UK: MQ Pub.

Fries, A. (2009). *Daydreams at work: Wake up your creative powers.* Sterling, VA: Capital Books.

Gale Reference Team. (2001). Daydreaming. *Gale Encyclopedia of Psychology.*

Glausiusz, J. (2014). *Living in an imaginary world.* https://www.scientificamerican.com/article/living-in-an-imaginary-world/

Klinger, E. (1990). *Daydreaming: Using waking fantasy and imagery for self-knowledge and creativity.* Los Angeles: Tarcher.

Lahey, J. (2013). Teaching kids to daydream. https://www.theatlantic.com/education/archive/2013/10/teach-kids-to-daydream/280615/

Lehrer, J. (2012). *The virtues of daydreaming.* http://www.newyorker.com/tech/frontal cortex/the-virtues-of-daydreaming.

Morris, T., Spittle, M., and Watt, A. (2005). *Imagery in sport.* Champaign, ILL: Human Kinetics.

Rossman, M. (2000). *Guided imagery for self-healing.* Novato, CA: New World Library.

Sheikh, A.A., & Shelkh, K.S. (eds) (1989). *Eastern & Western approaches to healing: Ancient wisdom and modern knowledge.* New York, NY: Wiley.

Siddle, B.K. (2008). *Sharpening the warrior's edge: The psychology of science and training.* Belleville, IL: PPCT Research Publications.

Singer, J. (1975). *The inner world of daydreaming.* New York, NY: Harper & Row.

Singer, J. (2009). Researching imaginative play and adult consciousness: Implications for daily and literary creativity. *Psychology of Aesthetics, Creativity, and the Arts* 3(4), 190-199.

Timothy A. Storlie, PhD

CHAPTER 2

BEFRIEND THE SUBCONSCIOUS MIND— THE SUPER INTELLIGENCE WITHIN

"The power to move the world is in the subconscious mind." – William James

In this Chapter

This chapter introduces you to the key player on the stage of transformational daydreaming—the subconscious mind. I don't know if the subconscious mind has the power to move *the* world as William James, the father of modern psychology, claimed in the quote above, but it certainly has the power to move *your* world.

The Super-Intelligence Within

Here are a few interesting facts about your soon-to-be new friend and advisor—the subconscious mind. This super intelligence within, is the overseer of your entire physical body—a body composed of approximately 37 trillion cells. It never sleeps, and is always on duty monitoring, maintaining, regulating, repairing, and healing the body. One of its most important functions (for purposes of this book), is to influence and direct your memory, intuition, dreaming, and daydreaming. Imagine such a friend!

As you study this chapter, remember to keep the key question in mind,

> *"How can I learn to communicate with my subconscious mind and daydream my way to a better life?"*

Be on the lookout for any information that might help answer your question.

Accelerated Learning — The Key Question

Each chapter includes these same suggestions for accelerating your learning, increasing comprehension and retention, and getting the most from this book. Begin each chapter by first turning to the end of the chapter so you can *preview* the list of main points. After completing your preview, then carefully *read* the chapter and complete each exercise.

As you study each chapter, read with the key question in mind. By keeping this key question in mind, you'll not only learn more, but you'll retain more of what you do learn. The overarching key question for *Part I* of this book is,

> *"How can I learn to communicate with my subconscious mind and daydream my way to a better life?"*

This book was written to help answer this important question. Finally, *review* what you learned by re-reading the list of main points. This process, faithfully followed, will help maximize your learning experience. Also, for your easy preview, review, and reference, you'll find a master list of the collective main points from each chapter located at the back of this book. More detailed suggestions on how to get the most from your learning efforts are offered in chapter 3.

How Big is One Trillion?

The subconscious mind directs the 37 trillion cells making up your physical body. In the United States, one trillion is 1,000 billion, written as a one with 12 zeros—1,000,000,000,000. Think about how large this number is.

Pretend you wanted to count to one trillion. Here's how long it would take you. If you counted by one's as fast as you could for 24 hours a day, 7 days a week, 52 weeks a year—never pausing—it would take you roughly 190,259 years to count to one trillion! And remember, your body has about 37 trillion cells. How long do you imagine it would take to count to 37 trillion? Counting at the same rate of speed (24 hours per day, non-stop, as described in the previous example), it would require approximately 7.4 million years to count all the cells in your body.

The point of this imaginary counting is this: try and imagine an overarching intelligence powerful enough to monitor and guide so many individual 37 trillion cells—this is your subconscious mind, your inner advisor. And, it gets even more amazing!

A study from Washington University, estimates there are about 100 trillion atoms in one human cell. That means you have 37 trillion cells in your body—every single one composed of 100 trillion atoms! Please pause and allow the magnitude of these numbers to sink in. Again, counting at the same non-stop rate of speed (as described previously, would require about 21 million years to count the atoms in just *one* cell of your body—just one of those 37 trillion.

How long would it take for you to count all the atoms in your body? Who the heck knows? It would take as long as it takes to count 21 million x 37 trillion. Whatever humongous number that adds up to, it's far too large for the conscious mind to grasp. But somehow, the subconscious mind has the capacity to oversee the work of every single atom—a mind-boggling ability! This is one reason why I labeled the subconscious mind as the super-intelligence that dwells within you.

Communication Between Conscious and Subconscious Mind

The subconscious mind controls and maintains your body. It also controls approximately 95% of everything that's goes on in your mind, including your thinking. Only about 5% is influenced or controlled by the conscious mind or personality.

No matter how conservatively you slice it, the subconscious mind is at least 1 million times more powerful than the conscious mind. And, as you'll learn in the following pages, the super intelligence of the subconscious mind seems willing (at least under certain circumstances) to communicate with the conscious mind. Gratitude would be an appropriate response.

Communication from the subconscious mind can take several

forms. Subconscious responses may come as thoughts, memories, images, symbols, sounds, silence, feelings, sensations, dreams, daydreams, and/or any combination of these experiences and others. Your role in this two-way communication process is to:

- Desire it.
- Intend to enter this type of respectful, practical relationship.
- Ask questions.
- Ponder and contemplate over your concerns.
- Sit expectantly and receptively, paying close attention to the responses of your subconscious mind.

Much more detailed information on how to do this is offered in later sections.

This communication between conscious mind and subconscious mind, is the core technique of the transformational daydreaming system. To ensure your success, it's important you thoroughly understand this concept. Your objective is to learn to communicate with the superintelligence within you—the subconscious mind—and to seek insight, understanding, creativity, and guidance that can be used to improve your personal and/or professional life. Here is an illustration of the 7-steps of Transformational Daydreaming. It summarizes the communication process between the conscious and subconscious mind.

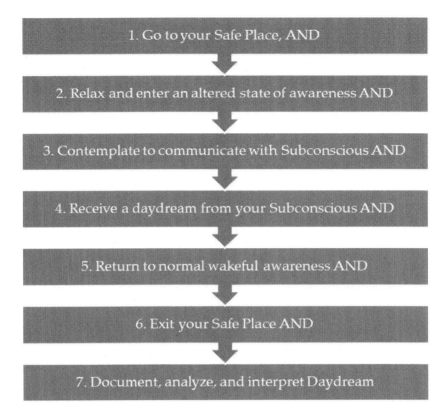

Please read through the above formula several times. This repetition will help create strong neural pathways in your brain making learning more rapid, deep, and permanent. (explained in chapter 3).

Repetition

As a former special education teacher, I appreciate the role of repetition and the value it brings to the learning process. For that reason, a significant amount of repetition is used throughout this book. As mentioned previously, this is done purposefully to help increase your understanding and retention of the information provided.

Please review this brief chapter on the subconscious mind several times. Be sure you understand what it is you're trying to do and how this process can help you achieve it. This will help build a useful, powerful view (explained in a later chapter). So, once again, the purpose of this program is help you:

> *Communicate consciously with the subconscious mind to receive guidance, insight, inspiration, and understanding to improve your personal and/or professional life.*

Exercise 1 – Befriend and Name the Subconscious Mind

The purpose of this exercise is for you to begin to befriend and name the subconscious mind. Carefully read through the information presented below and then complete the exercise. For purposes of this program, the subconscious mind is viewed as the friendly, super-intelligent elder that dwells with you—as an aspect of you—so in effect you will name a part of yourself.

1. Lie down. Get comfortable. Place one hand on your belly. Either hand is fine. Place the other hand on the back of your skull. Pretend you are talking with a new friend—your subconscious mind. The hand positions function like a confidential signal.

2. Close your eyes and continue this pretend conversation with your new friend. Express your gratitude for everything the elder subconscious mind has done and then politely ask for a more conscious relationship—a friendship. Example, *"Thank you for all you do to maintain a healthy body. I would enjoy developing a more conscious, cooperative, working relationship with you."* Pause and pay close attention. Be aware of any potential response from the subconscious mind. Remember, this response could come in the form of **thoughts, memories, images, symbols, sounds, silence, feelings, sensations, dreams, daydreams,**

and/or any combination of these experiences. At this point, you are not necessarily expected to receive a response, yet each person is unique, so who knows? It doesn't hurt to ask. Anything is possible.

3. Dive deep into your intuition (just intend it) and then bring back a name you feel is right for the subconscious (or ask it to provide a name). Don't worry. Relax. The name you select now is subject to later change based on your experience, guidance, and understanding. The point of naming the subconscious mind is simply to make it easier to hold conversations. A name you can call out to, for example, *"Charles,"* is more elegant and less cumbersome than saying, *"Hey subconscious mind."* Naming is mostly for your convenience. It helps make the concept of friendship more concrete and objective.

4. Use the selected name and continue talking to your elder subconscious mind. From this day forward, begin to think of your subconscious mind as a wise elder that you are developing a life-long friendship with.

5. Patiently cultivate a genuine, caring friendship by showing a friendly interest. For example, on a regular basis, take a few seconds to thank the subconscious mind for all it does. Imagine you are talking to an extremely powerful part of yourself that can do millions and billions of things at once. And, just as you don't call a friend on the phone each day to ask for a favor, refrain from doing this with the subconscious friend. It's fine to request an occasional favor. For example, try asking the subconscious mind to help relax the body when you are feeling stressed. You could also ask the subconscious to help you succeed with learning (and eventually mastering) all 7 steps of the transformational daydreaming program.

The Importance of Modifying Your Personal Point of View

Your worldview—beliefs and opinions about the "way things are"—is not set in stone. It is malleable and subject to modification, based on your experience and new learning (Feinstein & Krippner, 2006). For example, until recently, you may have believed it was impossible to develop a more conscious relationship with the subconscious mind. But now—based on new information provided in this book—you might be starting to consider that it may be possible. This change of mind is common and occurs naturally throughout the process of individual maturation over a lifetime. The accuracy of your personal narratives or worldview, has often been successfully challenged. The need for revision is frequent. Some of your views are challenged from biological, emotional, and mental growth. Others are challenged by exposure to new information, concepts, people, and specific circumstances that contradict the underlying premises of the stories. Examples: the tooth fairy, the Easter bunny, Santa Claus, listening to another's point of view and agreeing.

I encourage you to cultivate a view that fosters a conscious, respectful, working relationship with the subconscious mind. You can begin to develop this view by carefully completing the exercise above. The benefits of framing your relationship with the conscious mind in terms of friendship with a wise inner advisor, allows you to do what you already know how to do. You know how to make friends. Act friendly and be a friend. Make a new friend—the subconscious mind.

Here's the point: your worldview can shape what you believe is possible. Holding a view that frames friendship between conscious mind and subconscious mind as healthy and normal, helps it to be healthy and normal. In some way, your view functions as a self-fulfilling prophecy. Why? Because your view shapes your expectations of what is and is not possible. It seems as if expecting something to be possible, increases the likelihood that it is in fact possible. Your intentional framing of your relationship with the subconscious mind as a friendship, will help bring this friendship into actuality. Does that make sense? If not, pretend that it does.

Conclusion

As you begin to establish a closer, friendly relationship with your wise subconscious mind, you will probably experience certain events. Some might even be extraordinary. It matters how you categorize and assign meaning to these events. The specific category or meaning you assign can trigger which bio-chemicals are released into your body. The chemicals released into your body can determine whether your extraordinary experiences are felt as stressful or exciting.

Freeman and Lawlis (2001) describe the underlying mechanisms that explain how your view can impact your physiology. The model is quite complex but to put it simply, the three bodily systems involved are the nervous system, endocrine system, and immune system. These three systems communicate by using two pathways; the sympathetic-adrenal-medullary axis and the hypothalamic-pituitary-adrenal cortex axis which, in turn, use various messenger molecules to influence physiology.

The thoughts, feelings, and meaning you give to the concept of establishing friendship with your subconscious mind, triggers over 1,400 chemical reactions and over 30 hormones and neurotransmitters (Dawson, 2007). This overly-simplified explanation, outlines the physiological process by which your expectations and/or view can influence the body. The simple take-away is this,

---

Interpretation matters!
How you view something makes a difference.

The interpretation you give to an interaction with the subconscious mind, can play a significant role in how you will respond, and your responses can impact the future course of your relationship. How you interpret, judge, or explain experiences can directly influence physiology. What you imagine, believe, think, and say, matters (Kabat-Zinn, 1990).

In the next chapter, you'll learn advanced strategies to help you rapidly acquire the knowledge, understanding, experience, and skills necessary to receive maximum benefit from your studies, and (most importantly), to help you deepen your friendship with the subconscious mind.

List of Main Points for Preview and Review

- ✓ To accelerate your learning, increase comprehension and retention, and get the most from this book, begin each chapter by first turning to the end of the chapter so you can *preview* the list of main points. After completing your preview, then carefully *read* the chapter and complete each exercise. As you study each chapter, read with the key question in mind. Finally, *review* what you learned by re-reading the list of main points. Also, for your easy preview, review, and reference, you'll find a master list of the collective main points from each chapter located at the back of this book.

- ✓ This chapter introduced you to the subconscious mind — the super intelligence within you — that is at least one million times more powerful than the conscious mind.

- ✓ This super intelligence directs your memory, intuition, dreaming, and daydreaming; never sleeps; governs your body; and is always on duty monitoring, maintaining, regulating, repairing, and healing your body's 37 trillion cells — each cell composed of 100 trillion atoms.

- ✓ The subconscious mind seems willing to communicate with the conscious mind. This two-way communication is the core technique.

- ✓ Your objective is to learn to communicate with the superintelligence within you to seek insight, understanding, creativity, and guidance that can be used to improve your personal and professional life.

- ✓ Responses from the subconscious mind may come as thoughts, memories, images, symbols, sounds, silence, feelings, sensations, dreams, daydreams, and/or any combination of these experiences and others.

- ✓ Holding a view that frames friendship between conscious mind and subconscious mind as healthy and normal, helps it to be healthy and normal. The intentional framing of your relationship with the subconscious mind as friendship with an incredibly wise elder and inner advisor, will help bring this friendship into actuality.

- ✓ The thoughts, feelings, and interpretations you give to friendship with your subconscious mind, can trigger over 1,400 reactions from chemicals, hormones, and neurotransmitters. What you imagine, believe, think, and say, matters.

- ✓ The benefits of framing your relationship with the conscious mind in terms of friendship, allows you to do what you already know how to do, make friends.

- ✓ In exercise #1, the objective was to befriend and name the subconscious mind. The point of naming the subconscious mind is simply to make it easier to hold conversations.

References

Dawson, C. (2007). *The genie in your genes*. Santa Rosa, CA: Elite Books.

Feinstein, D., & Krippner, S. (2006). *The mythic path*. Santa Rosa, CA: Energy Psychology Press.

Freeman, L.W., & Lawlis, G.F. (2001). *Mosby's complementary and alternative medicine: A research-based approach*. St. Louis, MO: Mosby.

Kabat-Zinn (1990). *Full catastrophe living: Using the wisdom of your body and mind to face stress, pain, and illness*. New York, NY: Bantam Dell.

CHAPTER 3

ACCELERATED LEARNING

"The only person who is educated is the one who learned to learn and change." – Carl Rogers

In this Chapter

Chapter one provided an overview of *what* you could expect to learn from this program. This chapter offers suggestions on *how* you can accelerate your learning of the *what*.

Because many concepts explored here might be new to you, this chapter may prove a bit challenging. Rest assured, your efforts will be rewarded. The ideas and practices discussed in this chapter will be applicable—not only to your study and practice of transformational daydreaming—but to *any* topic of learning and/or skill development.

The Key Question

Each chapter includes the following suggestions for accelerating your learning, increasing comprehension and retention, and getting the most from this book.

1. Begin each chapter by first turning to the end of the chapter so you can *preview* the list of main points.
2. After completing your preview, then carefully *read* the chapter and complete each exercise.
3. As you study each chapter, read with the key question listed below in mind. By keeping this key question in mind, you'll not only learn more, but you'll retain more of what you do learn. The overarching key question for *Part I* of this book is,

"How can I learn to communicate with my subconscious mind and daydream my way to a better life?"

4. Finally, *review* what you learned by re-reading the list of main points.

This process, faithfully followed, will help maximize your learning experience. For your easy preview, review, and reference, you'll find a master list of the collective main points from each chapter located at the back of this book.

Develop Your Skills—the Big Idea

Communicating with the subconscious mind is a skill. To develop this skill (or any other), you must first desire it. If you identify your reasons for wanting to learn transformational daydreaming, this can enhance your motivation and quicken learning. The exercise below will help you identify your reasons.

Exercise

Look back over chapter one. Review the sample of applications and potential benefits of transformational daydreaming and then,

1. List what motivates you to *want* to learn and use the skills of transformational daydreaming. Reflect and ponder over your reasons. What is it that you hope to achieve from your mastery of these skills? For example: "I want to learn and use transformational daydreaming to enhance my creativity."

2. Save your list. Review it from time to time, especially if you need a quick reminder of what you're working toward and why.

> *Your learning, comprehension, and retention will always benefit when you have personally meaningful reasons for your studies.*

After igniting your desire to learn and listing your personal motivations, it's time to begin your disciplined course of study and practice. Wishing is not enough, but it begins with hope. True learning requires felt desire and deliberate doing. For best results, your approach to skill development should be grounded in:

- Principles of deep, deliberate practice (explained in the next section).

- An understanding of the role of multi-sensory mental imagery (explained in later chapters).
- Recognition and use of the 4-stage model for learning to achieve *conscious competence* (at a minimum) and hopefully, *unconscious competence*—concepts explained later in this chapter.

How to Achieve Excellence and/or Expertise

Hundreds of researchers have investigated the question, "what does it take to develop excellence and/or expertise in something" (Coyle, 2009). Yes, some people have more innate talent for a specific activity than others, but talent alone does not account for achieving excellence. What does? *Practice!*

Practice is the key. Practice is what is required to develop excellence and achieve expertise. But not just any kind of practice. The type of practice necessary for developing excellence and expertise is referred to as *deliberate practice* or *deep practice*.

Deep, Deliberate Practice

The collective findings of the studies mentioned above, point to the same conclusion—if you want to become an excellent performer of any type, you need to use deep, deliberate, accurate practice. Why? Because deep, deliberate practice speeds up and strengthens the creation of the brain's neural pathways. Neural pathways are involved in the creation of learning, memories and/or development of skills.

Once a neural circuit in the brain is formed, it tends to function as the default response for that specific skill. In other words, this circuit provides the "instructions" for how to carry out the task or skill. This is one reason it's important to practice a skill correctly right from the beginning. A neural pathway that has encoded memories of how to perform *incorrectly* can be difficult to change. It is certainly possible, but the point is, it's much easier to wire your learning correctly right from the start than it is to re-wire and correct the mistakes later.

Many individuals who eventually achieve excellence or expertise in a specific area, follow a similar learning strategy.

1. First, look at the whole, entire task to be learned. Get the "big picture." Then break the whole down into smaller, component parts. In terms of transformational daydreaming, this breakdown has already been done for you in the form of the 7-steps. For example: transformational daydreaming is the whole practice and each of the 7 steps are its smaller component parts.

2. Deliberately practice the component parts that make up the whole. Practice each component part until competent in that specific part. In terms of transformational daydreaming, this means you would practice each of the 7 steps (or part of a step) until, at a minimum, you feel competent. For example, you would first learn and practice how to physically relax and enter an altered state before moving on to the next step of contemplating.

3. After learning how to competently perform each of the smaller component parts, begin to link each previous part to the next part until you eventually connect all the individual links into one single whole. In terms of transformational daydreaming, this means you would practice each of the 7 steps (or part of a step) until you feel competent. For example, you would first learn and practice how to physically relax and enter an altered state. Then you would develop competence in contemplating before moving on to the next step of daydreaming. You would focus on progressively developing competence in each of the 7 steps of transformational daydreaming. You would link each current step to the next and so forth, until

you have finally integrated all the steps and component parts into one whole system.

Outline of Your Learning Cycle

At this point, it would be helpful for you to visualize your approximate learning cycle. Following this cycle will help further deepen, accelerate, and enhance your learning. Your cycle looks something like this:

1. Ignite your desire to learn transformational daydreaming.
2. Identify your motives for wanting to learn transformational daydreaming and for wanting to communicate with your subconscious mind.
3. Learn (and use) the basic principles of deep, deliberate accurate practice, and the 4-stage model of developing competence.
4. Continue to study the principles and practices of transformational daydreaming.
5. Use repetition and accurate practice to gain first-hand experience of each of the 7 steps of transformational daydreaming and begin to develop accurate, neural pathways.
6. Repeat the entire process over a long period of time to develop strong neural pathways, and achieve at least conscious competence (preferably mastery) in each of the skills of transformational daydreaming and integrate them into one, connected whole.

Does that make sense? Review and repeat. Review and repeat. Why? Because (as they say) repetition is the *Mother of Good Learning*.

The Mother of Good Learning—Repetition

Repetition is the mother of good learning. Why? Excellence and/or expertise is (in large part) dependent upon memory. As previously described, memory depends on a complex process involving the brain's neurons, neural pathways, and the coating of nerves with a substance called *myelin* (Whitmore, 2009). Apparently, it works something like this.

1. The more you practice—deeply, deliberately, and accurately—the more stable and strong your brain's neural pathways become.
2. The more you practice, the thicker the myelin sheath becomes.
3. The result of the above two, is a strong, accurate memory.
4. Learning, skill development, and achieving of excellence, require accurately encoded neural circuits, strengthened through repetition over time.

It seems that developing excellence and expertise is not just about repetition, myelin, and the 4-stages of competence. For many, there's another factor to consider—the fear of doing, the fear of failure.

Fear of Failure

As a psychologist, I understand you might feel a little hesitant over the *doing* phase. For most people, *doing* is the most challenging part of any learning process. Why? Because *doing* requires persistence and self-discipline. It tests your commitment.

There is also the commonly experienced *fear of failure.* Avoidance because of the fear of failure is so wide-spread, it's often viewed as a psychological defense mechanism—a mostly unconscious process developed to help protect you from the emotional pain of possible failure.

In the face of any hesitancy or fear of failure, you can benefit by reminding yourself that skill development, conscious communication with the subconscious mind, expansion of awareness, and the potential of expertise are close by—often just on the other side of fear and excuses. This book will help you move beyond fear of failing.

What You Can Expect

As you study and wrestle with the concepts presented, invest the time and effort required to complete all the exercises, and apply what you learn in daily life, you can expect to experience noticeable improvement in your ability to relax and enter an altered state of awareness. This enhanced ability to relax and enter an altered state should be welcomed as it indicates you are making good progress.

You can also expect to dramatically improve your contemplation skills—especially as you learn to use advanced, multi-sensory imagery. Most importantly, you can expect to increase your ability to befriend and communicate with the subconscious mind.

While you are working through the 7-steps of this program, you can track your progress through the four-stage model for developing competence (explained in the next section). I believe you'll find this four-stage model helpful as you explore the information and practices offered in the remainder of this book. And remember, this model is applicable to anything you are learning now, or anything you'll learn in the future.

The Four Stages of Developing Competence

When you undertake new learning or skill development, your progress follows a predictable trajectory moving through 4 main stages (Storlie, 2015). This new knowledge or skill could be anything from learning the transformational daydreaming process; learning to play a musical instrument; learning to speak a second language; or learning a martial art.

As you begin to study the transformational daydreaming program, your learning will unfold through these four stages as you move from the level of *beginner* toward the level of *mastery*. The four stages are:

Stage 1. Unconscious Incompetence

Stage 2. Unconscious Competence

Stage 3. Conscious Competence

Stage 4. Unconscious Competence

Stage 1: <u>Unconscious Incompetence</u>: This is the first stage of learning and developing competent skills. It is called *unconscious incompetence*. At this stage, you have little or no knowledge of the topic (you are unconscious) or the skills required for success (you are incompetent). In other words, you don't even know what you don't know and, you don't even know what you're supposed to be able to do, and can't do. Hence, the term *unconscious incompetence.*

To illustrate, I'll use learning to drive a car as an example. You want to learn to drive a car. You have no driving experience, no learner's permit, and no driver's license. You get behind the steering wheel of a car for the very first time in preparation for learning to drive.

At this stage, you are probably ignorant of the "big picture" — you know little or nothing about cars, about safe operation of a motor vehicle, about the rules of the road, and the hundreds of things you are expected to know, need to know, and may someday know. All you know for certain is that you want to learn to drive a car. You feel motivated. You daydream about driving a car and all the cool places you'll be able to go once you have a driver's license and your own car. Sound familiar?

This first learning stage is often quickly transcended by your growing realization that you "don't know," by thinking about your personal motivations for wanting to learn to drive, and by your willingness to receive instructions and corrective feedback from an experienced, licensed driver. Transcending the first stage is also helped by exposure to new information, from practice, from your experience of many small successes, and from receiving positive feedback and encouragement.

In terms of transformational daydreaming, this stage describes the person who has rarely or never thought about how to use daydreaming to communicate with the subconscious mind. Perhaps the person has never even considered the possibility that such communication was possible. Similar to the new driver described above, the first-stage learner of transformational daydreaming is largely unaware of the "big picture," ignorant of how to organize the overall learning experience, doesn't know where to begin, and doesn't know what questions to ask. The first-stage learner is unaware of common mistakes and of helpful practices, and is largely in the dark about what to expect and when.

Both the person new to transformational daydreaming (as well as the new driver) can expect—with personal motivation, persistent effort, exposure to accurate information, appropriate personal reflection, corrective feedback, encouragement, and successful practice—to evolve from the first stage of *unconscious incompetence* to the second stage of learning—developing *conscious incompetence*. Please spend a few minutes reflecting on your own first-level experience of learning something new.

Stage 2: <u>Conscious Incompetence</u>: This is the second stage of learning and developing competent skills. It is called *conscious incompetence*. You have developed very basic knowledge of the topic (conscious) but are unable to adequately perform the skills (incompetence). In other words, you are now aware of what you don't yet know, and, you also know what you're supposed to be able to do but can't. Hence, the term *conscious incompetence*.

Continue with the example of learning to drive a car. You wanted to learn to drive a car. You did what was required, learned something about the big picture of driving, safe operation of a motor vehicle, rules of the road, and all the other things required to earn your learner's permit (conscious). You cannot yet drive independently, but you can drive with appropriate supervision. You are clearly making progress. Not only have you begun to accumulate knowledge of your topic and understanding of the skills required for success, but now you also realize how much more there is to learn and which skills need further development. In other words, you know what you know and what you can't do. You are consciously incompetent (at this stage).

In terms of transformational daydreaming, this stage describes the person who has studied the book, developed basic knowledge, and is beginning to explore how to communicate with the subconscious mind (conscious). Although the person is experimenting with the practices, he or she is unable to consistently communicate with the subconscious mind (incompetence). Hence, the term *conscious incompetence.*

At this second stage, both the transformational daydreamer and the new driver have made clear progress. They both knew what they wanted and they went for it. Both did what was required, learned something about the big picture, and have taken up practice in earnest. Yet, each has further work to do before they will experience consistent, independent success. Both can expect—with proper motivation, persistent effort, continued learning, appropriate personal reflection, corrective feedback, encouragement, and successful practice—to evolve from the second stage of *conscious incompetence* to the third stage of learning—*conscious competence*. Please spend a few minutes reflecting on your own second-level experience of learning something new.

Stage 3: <u>Conscious Competence</u>: This is the third stage of learning and developing competence. It is called *conscious competence* because at this point you have developed knowledge of the topic (conscious) and are now able to adequately perform the skills (competence). At this stage, skills must be purposefully and mindfully evoked. The skills are not yet developed enough to be automatic. You know what you know and you can do what is required, but only on-purpose, with thoughtful attention. You cannot yet perform what is required automatically and without thinking about it first. Hence, the term *conscious competence.*

To continue with the example of driving a car: you now have your driver's license. You have made significant progress and, as a result, can drive independently. You realize that in the years to come, you will continue to deepen your learnings and improve your skills.

In terms of transformational daydreaming, this stage describes the person who has completed the program, developed an adequate knowledge base, consistently experimented with the suggested practices, and as a result, is now enjoying more consistent, satisfying, and rewarding communication with the subconscious mind. At this stage, the skills of transformational daydreaming are not yet automatic. They must be purposefully and mindfully carried out.

At this third stage, both the transformational daydreamer and the newly-licensed driver have made substantial progress. Both completed the requisite study and practice, and as a result, are now enjoying the fruits of their labors. Yet, each will require much more practice before they will experience consistent, automatic success. Both can hope that with continued motivation, persistence, learning, feedback, personal reflection, and successful practice over a long period of time, to evolve from the third stage of *conscious competence* to the fourth and final stage of learning— *unconscious competence*—perhaps even mastery! Please spend a few minutes reflecting on your own third-level experience of learning something new.

Stage 4: <u>Unconscious Competence</u>: This is the fourth and final stage of learning and developing competence. This is the beginning level of expertise where your knowledge and skills are available automatically. It is called *unconscious competence* because at this point you have developed significant knowledge, understanding, and deep experience of the topic. You know what you know without having to think about it (unconscious), and you can do what is required automatically without having to think about it first (competence).

Whether communicating with the subconscious mind or driving a car, you can perform it expertly without apparent conscious thinking or effort (unconscious). It's as if you can do it automatically (competence). This stage indicates a very high level of achievement and few will attain it. For many skills, achieving third-level competence is adequate. Probably the most common area where people achieve unconscious competence is in driving a car.

Imagine you have been driving a car for many years. What initially was confusing, is now comfortable. What was initially challenging (tasks requiring focused, one-pointed concentration) is now automatic and effortless. There was a time when you could barely keep in mind all the things you had to do and pay attention to in order to drive a car. But now, you can safely drive down the freeway at 70 MPH, while listening to soft music, visiting with a passenger, and enjoying the passing scenery—something almost unimaginable only a few short years before. You may never develop the driving skills of a professional race-car driver, but you can safely guide your vehicle almost effortlessly to wherever your destination may be.

Whether communicating with the subconscious mind or driving your car, this is the stage where you can apply your knowledge and skills with little or no conscious effort. You have reached a beginning level of expertise. No small achievement! Your practice flows automatically out of the depths of hard-earned experience and deep knowing. Although this is not the end of learning—because there is no end to learning—it is, to use a martial arts concept, the black-belt level where mastery begins.

In many ways, you will always be a learner, but at this level, you may also be considered a role model and teacher. Although this is the final stage in this model, further progress is possible depending on your intention, motivation, and dedication. Once you develop expertise, you can always develop a little more, then a little more, then a little more after that. After all, where is the end to learning?

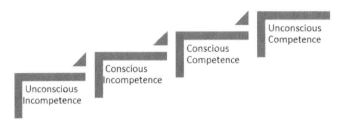

The Importance of Your Personal Point of View

In addition to making use of the 4-stage model of learning, you are encouraged to purposefully cultivate a specific point of view—an informed opinion that supports your respectful friendship and working relationship with the subconscious mind. Why? Because your view impacts your physiology and this can influence your rate of learning and progress. More on this later.

Your view can be understood as the collective total of your assumptions, beliefs, and interpreted experiences (Storlie, 2015). Consisting of beliefs, feelings, and rules, your conscious interpretation, and the meaning you give to your experience, can all shape and modify existing views. In other words, your personal point of view functions similarly to a filter. This filter colors or influences how you perceive and make sense of personal experience.

This is an important consideration when you desire to deepen your relationship with the subconscious mind. Here's why.

Because the brain uses this view as it works to identify, categorize, explain, predict, and interpret daily experiences (Feinstein & Krippner, 2006), it is helpful to cultivate a view that embraces the underlying principles of transformational daydreaming. These principles include the important concepts of contemplation, altered states of awareness, and the role and power of your subconscious mind. The view you adopt to explain the process of communication between your conscious mind and subconscious mind should make sense to you and be meaningful and important to you. Reviewing the first three chapters of this book from time to time can be helpful in this regard.

Thankfully, your worldview is not set in stone. It is malleable and subject to modification, based on experience and new learning (Feinstein & Krippner, 2006). For example: until recently, you may have believed it was impossible to develop a more conscious relationship with the subconscious mind. But now—based on new information provided in chapter 1 and 2, you may be thinking it's possible. This change of mind is common and occurs quite naturally throughout the process of education, aging, and maturation. For example, Santa Claus, hearing the other side of an argument, moving away from your parent's home for the first time, etc.

Here's the main point:

> *Your view can shape your interpretations of experience, thoughts, and—from the choices made—influence behavior.*

Freeman and Lawlis (2001) describe the underlying mechanisms by which your self-talk, and mental or narrative interpretation can impact your physiology. The three systems involved in this communication process are the nervous system, endocrine system, and immune system.

Dawson (2007) goes into considerable detail explaining how your body responds to your thoughts and feelings. He suggests there are over 1,400 chemical reactions and over 30 hormones and neurotransmitters that can shift in response to perceived stressful stimuli. This overly-simplified explanation, outlines the process by which your thoughts influence the body.

Conclusion

The take-away is this:

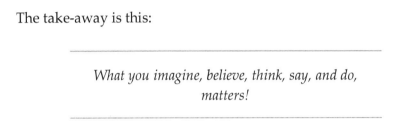

What you imagine, believe, think, say, and do, matters!

The interpretation you give to an interaction can play a significant role in how your body will respond. Interpretation matters!

List of Main Points for Preview and Review

- ✓ To accelerate your learning, increase comprehension and retention, and get the most from this book, begin each chapter by first turning to the end of the chapter so you can *preview* the list of main points. After completing your preview, then carefully *read* the chapter and complete each exercise. As you study each chapter, read with the key question in mind. Finally, *review* what you learned by re-reading the list of main points. Also, for your easy preview, review, and reference, you'll find a master list of the collective main points from each chapter located at the back of this book.

- ✓ Communicating with the subconscious mind is a skill.

- ✓ Write down the reasons you want to learn transformational daydreaming. This can enhance motivation and quicken learning. Save this list and review it from time to time.

- ✓ Begin a disciplined course of study. Wishing is not enough. True learning requires desiring and *doing*.

- ✓ For most people, *doing* is the most challenging part of the learning process. *Doing* requires persistence and self-discipline.

- ✓ Practice is the key. Your practice should be grounded in the principles of deep, deliberate, accurate practice, and informed by an understanding of the role of repetition, neural pathways, and myelin.

- ✓ Avoidance in trying something new because of a fear of failure is viewed as a psychological defense mechanism designed to help protect you from the emotional pain of possible failure.

- ✓ Remind yourself that skill development, conscious communication with the subconscious mind, expansion of awareness, and the potential of expertise are often experienced just on the other side of fear and excuses.

- ✓ Invest the time and effort required to complete all the exercises.

- ✓ Expect to experience noticeable improvement in your ability to relax and enter an altered state of awareness, to increase contemplation skills, use of multi-sensory imagery, and to increase your ability to befriend and communicate with the subconscious mind.

- ✓ Your learning of transformational daydreaming will unfold through four stages as you move from beginner toward the level of mastery. These four stages are unconscious incompetence, conscious incompetence, conscious competence, and unconscious competence.

- ✓ In your study and practice of transformational daydreaming, you want to achieve *conscious competence* (at the minimum) and hopefully, *unconscious competence*.

- ✓ You will always be a learner. Once you develop expertise, you can develop a little more, then a little more, then a little more after that.

- ✓ Purposefully cultivate a point of view that supports your respectful friendship and working relationship with the subconscious mind.

- ✓ Cultivate a view that embraces the underlying principles of transformational daydreaming, especially the important concepts of contemplation, altered states of awareness, and the role and power of your subconscious mind.

- ✓ There are over 1,400 chemical reactions and over 30 hormones and neurotransmitters that can shift in response to your mental interpretations.

- ✓ Your interpretation matters!

References

Coyle, D. (2009). *The talent code.* New York, NY: Bantam Books.

Dawson, C. (2007). *The genie in your genes.* Santa Rosa, CA: Elite Books.

Feinstein, D., & Krippner, S. (2006). *The mythic path.* Santa Rosa, CA: Energy Psychology Press.

Freeman, L.W., & Lawlis, G.F. (2001). *Mosby's complementary ann alternative medicine: A research-based approach.* St. Louis, MO: Mosby.

Storlie, T. (2015). *Person-centered communication with older adults.* San Diego, CA: Academic Press.

Whitmore, P.G. (2009). A new mindset for a new mind: understanding new theories about how the brain works, and what it can mean for adult learning. *American Society for Training and Development. T + D,* 60-65, http://www.astd.org.

CHAPTER 4

ALL ABOUT DAYDREAMING— EXPAND YOUR VIEW

Daydreaming is a multi-sensory language used by your subconscious mind to communicate with you.

In this Chapter

This chapter was written to expand your understanding and appreciation of daydreams and daydreaming, and help build your view. Greater understanding of some of the details of daydreaming can help you more easily unlock the door leading to a friendly relationship with the subconscious mind.

What is a daydream? Why do you daydream? What triggers daydreaming? How often do you daydream? How long are your daydreams? What do you daydream about? Do your nighttime dreams and daydreams share any common characteristics? These are some of the important questions explored in this chapter. The answers to these questions shed light on the special language used by your wise, elder advisor (your subconscious mind).

The Key Question — Again

Each chapter includes repetition of key concepts and these same suggestions as a way to accelerate your learning, increase comprehension and retention, and help you get the most from this book.

1. Begin each chapter by first turning to the end of the chapter so you can *preview* the list of main points.
2. After completing your preview, then carefully *read* the chapter and complete each exercise.
3. As you study each chapter, read with the key question in mind. By keeping this key question in the forefront of your mind, you'll not only learn more, but you'll retain more of what you do learn. The overarching key question for *Part I* of this book is,

"How can I learn to communicate with my subconscious mind and daydream my way to a better life?"

4. Finally, *review* what you learned by re-reading the list of main points.

This process, faithfully followed, will help maximize your learning experience. For your easy preview, review, and reference, you'll find a master list of the collective main points from each chapter located at the back of this book.

What is Daydreaming?

Daydreaming is an expression of your imagination. It's a dream-like stream of imagery that you experience while awake or semi-awake (Klinger, 1990). In this book, daydreaming is viewed as the language of the subconscious mind as it attempts to communicate with you. This language is multi-sensorial and sends messages to you, the conscious personality. Daydreaming is known by many names—*mind-wandering, mental reverie, waking fantasy,* and *mental rehearsal.* Other terms used include: *contemplation, reverie,* and *visualization.*

Why do you Daydream?

Daydreaming is often viewed as the default position of the brain (Singer, 2009). This means that when your conscious mind is not busy with daily activities, the brain often reverts (or defaults) to daydreaming. That's why daydreaming is considered the brain's default position.

Evidence from neuroscience research suggests that your attention to the outside world waxes and wanes throughout the day—it increases and decreases (Smallwood, Beach, Schooler, & Handy, 2008). During those times—when your attention to the external, outside world increases—your awareness of the internal, inside world decreases.

Conversely, when your awareness of the outer world decreases, your awareness of the inner world increases. In other words, when your conscious mind becomes more quiet, your subconscious mind becomes more active, and it communicates with you via daydreaming. It's communicating, but are you paying attention? It might be giving you insightful and important information. This course will teach you how to do that in a special way. Please reflect on this concept for a couple minutes.

Research suggests something else of interest—daydreaming is generated in many of the same areas of the brain that would show activity if the experience you are daydreaming about was physically occurring (Klinger, 1990). It is common knowledge that skills improve with practice. Brain findings such as these, help explain why mental rehearsal and daydreaming can also help improve physical skills and performance. This is the type of information that can help shape and influence your developing view of daydreaming.

Who Daydreams?

You daydream. I daydream. Basically, everyone daydreams. Daydreaming is a normal human activity (Rao, 2002). Many contemporary psychologists view daydreaming as normal, natural, and healthy, unless it chronically interferes with daily living (Gayle Group, 2001).

When do you Daydream?

Studies show that you are more likely to daydream:

- When you feel bored.
- When you're not interested or involved in what you're doing.
- When the things you are doing demand little conscious focus or concentration.

There's at least one other time when you're likely to daydream—at certain points in the 90-minute cycle of brain activity. Apparently, the brain operates on 90-minute cycles throughout the day and night (Gayle Group, 2001). This implies that waking-thought and daydreaming, and sleeping-thought and night dreaming, are more alike than different (Klinger, 1990).

How Long are Your Daydreams?

Most daydreams are short, averaging from a few seconds to a couple of minutes in length (Fries, 2009). Researchers estimate that you spend anywhere from 30% to 70% of your waking hours in various kinds of daydreaming or mind-wandering. It seems the subconscious mind is communicating with you for a large percentage of each day. But again, the question is, are you paying attention?

What do You Daydream About?

Most daydreams reflect whatever is uppermost on your mind, e.g., preoccupation with concerns, desires, fantasies, feelings, goals, hopes, memories, plans, wishes and worries (Baruss, 2003). You tend to daydream about the circumstances, events, or memories that have the most immediate emotional impact on you.

Broadly speaking, mental wandering is daydreaming. Contemplating is daydreaming. Thinking about old boyfriends or old girlfriends is daydreaming. Reminiscing over memories is daydreaming. And through your dreams and daydreams, the subconscious mind communicates with you about your desires, fears, what you've learned from the past, what you anticipate from the future, and even what you may not want to know (Baruss, 2003).

How does Daydreaming Affect the Body?

Daydreaming makes use of mental imagery. The use of mental imagery can result in physiological, biochemical, and emotional changes in the body (review chapter 3). Mental imagery activates relevant behavioral, cognitive, neurological and other physiological processes. Why? Because of a process referred to as *functional equivalence*.

The concept of *functional equivalence* suggests that mental rehearsal or daydreaming about something is functionally equivalent to performing the physical activity (Murphy, 2005). For example, research shows that when you are daydreaming about lifting weights, you experience some of the same measurable benefits that you would if physically lifting weights. This benefit seems to hold true for the practice of any sport or physical activity, e.g., martial arts, dancing, basketball, jogging, tennis, etc. It also applies to social interactions, conversations, job interviews and the like. The concept of functional equivalence suggests that imagining yourself completing 20 karate kicks and 30 karate strikes offers at least some of the same benefits as if you had physically done them. It also implies that imagining talking with your boss triggers many of the same physical and emotional responses that would occur if you were physically meeting with him/her.

Imagery's effect on the body is well documented (Freeman & Lawlis, 2001). This means that the brain uses some of the same neural pathways while daydreaming as it does when you're physically doing the activity. This information has many practical applications. Again, the important point is this:

Daydreaming is (to some degree) functionally equivalent to physically doing the activity.

Types of Daydreaming—Spontaneous and Intentional

There are two main types of daydreaming— *intentional daydreaming* and *spontaneous daydreaming* (Klinger, 1990). The system taught in this book, makes use of both types—using intentional contemplation to trigger spontaneous daydreams. Spontaneous daydreaming is unplanned, unintended daydreaming. It is not something that you consciously decide to do. Spontaneous daydreaming is the product of your subconscious mind. It is often triggered by memories, feelings, and circumstances. It's also known as mind-wandering or waking fantasy.

Intentional daydreaming is planned, purposeful daydreaming. It is something you consciously decide to do. Intentional daydreaming is initiated by will, desire, and decision. This type of daydreaming is often used in personal growth, psychotherapy, counseling, sports, and business. It's also referred to as directed daydreaming, guided imagery, mental rehearsal, and visualization. As previously explained, this book presents a hybrid process for intentionally triggering spontaneous daydreams.

Exercise - What Have You Been Daydreaming About?

Put on your detective's hat. Investigate your daydreaming experiences a little. Try to identify your daydreaming patterns and triggers. Who knows? You may be able to use the patterns you discover to help you develop your skills. Investigate and document:

- What time or times of the day do you most often daydream?
- Where are you physically when you are daydreaming?
- What are you usually doing just before you begin to daydream?
- How vivid are your daydreams?
- What seems to trigger your daydreaming? Is it because you feel bored? Is it because you're not involved in what you're doing? Is it because you want to be somewhere else? What is your best guess?

Reflect on whether daydreams have ever helped you solve a problem. If so, this is an example of the subconscious mind — your inner, elder advisor — communicating with you to help with a concern.

Transformational Daydreaming to Communicate with the Subconscious Mind

Repetition is the mother of learning. This is another description of the core communication process you will use throughout the remainder of this book. Understanding it will help you.

1. You begin with a hope, desire, or need for information, insight, and inspiration about a specific concern, issue, or problem.

2. Sitting in a relaxed, altered state of awareness, you communicate your desire to the subconscious mind using multi-sensory contemplation — a pictorial language that it can understand. This contemplation is how you "ask" the subconscious mind for a helpful daydream related to your desire, problem, or concern.

3. When you want to communicate with the subconscious mind, you use contemplation. When the subconscious mind wants to communicate with you, it uses spontaneous daydreams.

In other words, it's as if you're asking the subconscious mind for help. The method you are using to ask for help is contemplation. Your subconscious mind—the super intelligence within you—is able to help and willing to communicate with you. The method the subconscious mind uses to respond to you is through the use of memories, thoughts, feelings, images, symbols, sensations, and sounds—in other words, daydreaming.

This two-way communication between conscious mind and subconscious mind is the core technique of this system. You use this system to seek insight, information, understanding, creativity and guidance from the super intelligence within to improve your personal and professional life. You contemplate to open the line of communication from you to your subconscious and then you wait for a response in the form of a spontaneous daydream.

When Confusion Arises

This course contains a lot of new information—it's a bit overwhelming! Here are some ways to help reduce confusion. Confusion is normal—a sign of new learning. Confusion is not a signal to quit. It's your brain suggesting it might be helpful if you slow down, take a fresh look at the information, ponder over the concepts, and then review or re-read as necessary. Once confusion is resolved, you'll feel comfortable, confident, and ready to move ahead. Yes, it's usually best if you clearly understand each step before proceeding but not always—perfection isn't required. Some learners will do better (despite confusion) if they plunge ahead and complete the program. Do what's best for you. But whatever you do, don't let confusion tempt you to make excuses, lose interest, and quit!

> *Repetition is the mother of good learning.*

Read, review, and practice. Read, review, and practice. Work the system. As my martial arts teacher said, *"the secret to mastery is this—if you practice very hard, you'll become very good!"*

Conclusion

Congrats! You've finished chapters 1-4. Along the way, you built a conceptual and theoretical foundation—a view. From this point forward—as you continue your march toward conscious competence and beyond—the emphasis is on *doing*.

In the next chapter—before you start contemplating—you'll learn step one of the transformational daydreaming system. This means you'll learn how to go to your inner Safe Place.

List of Main Points for Preview and Review

- ✓ To accelerate your learning, increase comprehension and retention, and get the most from this book, begin each chapter by first turning to the end of the chapter so you can *preview* the list of main points. After completing your preview, then carefully *read* the chapter and complete each exercise. As you study each chapter, read with the key question in mind. Finally, *review* what you learned by re-reading the list of main points. Also, for your easy preview, review, and reference, you'll find a master list of the collective main points from each chapter located at the back of this book.

- ✓ Daydreaming is commonly viewed by most as normal, healthy, and natural.

- ✓ As far as anyone knows, everyone daydreams.

- ✓ Daydreaming is probably the brain's automatic or default activity when attention to the external world is reduced.

- ✓ Daydreaming occurs about every 90 minutes, much like the cycle of nighttime dreaming.

- ✓ Most daydreams are relatively short, averaging from a few seconds to a couple of minutes.

- ✓ Most people's daydreams reflect their preoccupation with current concerns, desires, fantasies, feelings, hopes, goals, and worries.

- ✓ Other popular terms for daydreaming include mind-wandering or waking fantasy.

- ✓ There are two types of daydreaming: intentional and spontaneous daydreaming.

- ✓ It's important to identify your daydreaming patterns and trigger.

- ✓ The core technique of this system is the two-way communication between the conscious mind and the subconscious mind. You use this system to seek insight, information, understanding, creativity, and guidance from the super intelligence within to improve your personal and professional life. It's as if you're asking the subconscious mind for help. The method you are using to ask for help is contemplation. Your subconscious mind—the super intelligence within you—is able and willing to communicate with you. The method the subconscious mind uses to respond to you is through the use of memories, thoughts, feelings, images, symbols, sensations, and sounds—daydreaming.

- ✓ Consider keeping a daydreaming journal.

References

Baruss, I. (2003). Alterations of consciousness: An empirical analysis for social scientists. Washington, D.C.: American Psychological Association.

Freeman, L.W., & Lawlis, G.F. (2001). *Mosby's complementary and alternative medicine: A research-based approach*. St. Louis, MO: Mosby.

Fries, A. (2009). *Daydreams at work: Wake up your creative powers*. Sterling, VA: Capital Books.

Gale Reference Team. (2001). Daydreaming. Gale Encyclopedia of Psychology.

Klinger, E. (1990). *Daydreaming: Using waking fantasy and imagery for self-knowledge and creativity*. Los Angeles: Tarcher.

Murphy, S. (2005). *The sport psychology handbook.* Champaign, IL: Human Kinetics.

Rao, R.K. (2002). *Consciousness Studies: Cross-cultural perspectives*. Jefferson, NC: McFarland & Co.

Singer, J. (2009). Researching imaginative play and adult consciousness: Implications for daily and literary creativity. Psychology of Aesthetics, Creativity, and the Arts 3(4), 190-199.

Smallwood, J., Beach, E., Schooler, J.W., & Handy, T.C. (2008). Going AWOL in the brain: Mind wandering reduces cortical analysis of external events. Journal of Cognitive Neuroscience 20(3), 458-469.

CHAPTER 5

TRANSFORMATIONAL DAYDREAMING STEP 1—GO TO YOUR SAFE PLACE

It began with hope—your hope to create a better life. Acting on that hope, you began study of this book. You began to explore how daydreaming could help transform your hopes and dreams into actual experience. Your preparation as an apprentice daydreamer is almost complete. What was once hope is nearing actuality.

In chapters 1-4, you read the theories, reviewed the facts, considered the arguments, and completed the exercises. Along the way, you expanded your understanding and deepened your appreciation of the inner universe of daydreaming. Most importantly, you began to cultivate a special friendship—a conscious, respectful, working relationship with your subconscious mind—the super intelligence that dwells within you.

You've completed the foundational work necessary for building a useful and useable view. You're making good progress! From this point forward, the emphasis shifts from developing a theoretical *view*, to the practical work of *doing*—of translating theory into practice. This is the next important step in developing *conscious competence* within the Transformational Daydreaming process.

In the coming chapters, you will learn to select and name your Safe Place, to relax deeply, to enter an altered state of awareness, and contemplate. Most importantly, you will learn that when you want to communicate with the subconscious mind, you use contemplation, and when the subconscious mind wants to communicate with you, it uses spontaneous daydreams.

Transformational daydreaming is a special way of using the power of your imagination to develop a working relationship between the conscious mind and the subconscious mind. All the remaining details of how to do this will be explained in these final chapters.

In this Chapter

In this chapter, you'll learn how to do step 1 the 7-step program. Your first objective will be to imagine your inner *Safe Place* (Storlie, 2015). This is a special mental place where you can go any time you want or need to become deeply relaxed.

Step 2 is explained in the next chapter. There you will to learn to enter an altered state of awareness. Later, you will use this altered state to begin communicating with the subconscious mind—a goal discussed repeatedly throughout this book.

Deep Learning, Deep Practice, and a New Key Question

Here they are again, the purposeful repetition of important concepts and suggestions for accelerating your learning, increasing comprehension and retention, and getting the most from this book.

As always, you should begin each chapter by first turning to the end of the chapter so you can *preview* the list of main points. After completing your preview, then carefully *read* the chapter and complete each exercise.

Finally, *review* what you learned by re-reading the list of main points. This process, faithfully followed, will help maximize your learning experience. Also, for your easy preview, review, and reference, you'll find a master list of the collective main points from each chapter located at the back of this book.

As you study this chapter, read with the key question in mind. But wait. Something is different. Since you completed the *theoretical* Part I of this book and are now entering the *practice* phase, your key question needs to reflect this change. The overarching key question for the remainder of this book is now,

"How can I use transformational daydreaming to help me _____ ?"

You'll notice the final part of the question is blank. Here's why. From now on, when you are faced with a concern, question, or problem that could benefit from the insights provided by the subconscious mind, you can ask this question and fill in the missing part with whatever your specific concern might be. For example: *how can I use transformational daydreaming to help me improve my physical health and wellness? How can I use transformational daydreaming to help me improve my marriage? How can I use transformational daydreaming to help me improve my skills in the martial arts?*

Whatever issue you face—physical, emotional, social, financial, mental, personal, professional, religious, psychic, transpersonal, or spiritual—you can use the same empowering question to orient your view and thought process in a solution-focused direction. Using the transformational daydreaming process, the focus is on *doing*. What can you *do* about your concern?

Introduction to Your Safe Place

To succeed with transformational daydreaming, you need to be able to deeply relax (Rossman, 2000). This is an important prerequisite requirement. Please take your time when practicing relaxation techniques. Feeling rushed, impatient, or in a hurry will make it nearly impossible to relax, and much more difficult to enter an altered state of awareness. Relaxation is a skill you'll use and value for the rest of your life. Stress, tension, and worry impede your critical thinking and reasoning as well as your creative process. The time you spend learning how to improve your ability to relax will pay big dividends in nearly every arena of your life.

Someday you'll be able to quickly relax or daydream just about anywhere. But—at this stage of your developing competence—for best results, it's helpful to practice relaxation techniques in a special setting, your Safe Place.

Your Safe Place is somewhere where you can feel safe, comfortable, and relaxed.

You can think of your Safe Place as your base camp or staging area for relaxing, contemplating, meditating, and daydreaming. Your vivid imagination is the key that grants entry into this mental staging area.

With intentional, regular, and repeated practice, your Safe Place will begin to function as an automatic trigger. This means you'll be able to quickly relax and enter an altered state of awareness simply by going there.

Your objective in step one is to locate, remember, or imagine your Safe Place, and begin to use it as directed. Here's how to do it.

Transformational Daydreaming—Step 1: Go to Your Safe Place

Your Safe Place is somewhere where you feel safe, comfortable, and relaxed. But, before you can use your Safe Place, you must first locate and select it. You have three possible options. Review all three options and then select the best option for you.

Option one: your Safe Place might be an actual physical place where you have free and easy access. For example, a favorite chair located in your home. In this case, you could physically sit (or visualize) resting in your favorite chair when practicing your relaxation techniques and/or conducting transformational daydreaming.

Option two: your Safe Place might be an actual physical place but it's only easily accessible through memory. For example, a secluded ocean cove where you once sat to contemplate. In this case, you could recall a memory of your visit to this cove and visualize sitting in the sand to practice your relaxation techniques and/or conducting transformational daydreaming.

Option three: your Safe Place is an actual physical place or an imagined place where you have never been, accessible only via your imagination. For example, you saw a picture of a hammock hung between two trees in a mountain meadow. You've never been there. In this case, you would imagine resting comfortably in the hammock when practicing your relaxation techniques and/or conducting transformational daydreaming.

Whether your Safe Place is an actual place, the memory of an actual place you have been, or a place you made up in your imagination, identify and name it now. You might want to try out several names and then choose the one that feels best. The overarching guideline is this:

Your Safe Place is somewhere you feel safe, comfortable, and relaxed.

Exercise—Identify and Name Your Safe Place

Slowly reflect over your three options for a Safe Place. Make a list of possibilities. When you're ready, use your imagination to briefly visit each possibility. After your exploration, select the option you feel is best for you. This is your Safe Place—where you feel safe, relaxed, and comfortable.

It's important that you name your Safe Place. Naming your Safe Place will help you to be able to access it more quickly. This should be a name you can easily recall—a name that helps trigger activation of the memory and feeling of being there. Example: *"Hawaiian Safe Place,"* or *"Meditation Chair."*

Once you've selected and named your Safe Place, close your eyes and relax. Using your imagination, mentally go to your Safe Place, sit down and begin to feel more relaxed. Imagine your Safe Place with as much rich and vivid detail as you can. Repeat its name three times and pretend you are there now. Slow down mentally. Pay attention. What do you sense about your Safe Place? What do you see? How does being there make you feel? Take your time. There's no hurry and there's no pressure.

Now, to make it much easier to return to your Safe Place whenever you wish, do the following. Continue sitting in your Safe Place with your eyes closed. Mentally suggest the following to yourself at least 5-6 times,

> *"I can visit my Safe Place whenever I want. I simply mentally repeat its name 3 times, imagine being there, and think the phrase 'safe, comfortable, and relaxed.'"*

When it comes to learning, suggestion, and retention, remember repetition is your friend. You are encouraged to repeat this exercise several times and to use suggestions from chapter 3 to help accelerate and deepen your learning experience. Use what you learned about deep, deliberate practice to strive toward conscious competency. You want to be able to access this state quickly and to feel safe, comfortable, and relaxed.

> *Your Safe Place is an important, beneficial technique you can use for the rest of your life.*

Your Safe Place. It's where you can go anytime you want to feel safe, comfortable, and relaxed. It's where you can go to take a mental break from stress and/or to contemplate, meditate, and communicate with the subconscious mind. In the next section, you'll learn more about the many uses of your Safe Place.

Three Main Uses for Your Safe Place

There are at least three main uses for your Safe Place. You may discover others.

1. You can use your Safe Place to relax whenever you need to.
2. You can use your Safe Place to contemplate and/or explore any of the more than 37 applications of daydreaming described in chapter 10.
3. You can use your Safe Place to communicate with the Subconscious Mind to seek advice, counsel, and insight into any question, concern, or problem.

Conclusion

You learned step 1 of the 7-step transformational daydreaming system. You were shown how to go to your Safe Place. In the next chapter, you'll learn step 2—how to use the countdown to relaxation method and enter and deepen your altered state.

List of Main Points for Preview and Review

✓ Begin each chapter by first turning to the end of the chapter so you can *preview* the list of main points. After completing your preview, then carefully *read* the chapter and complete each exercise. Finally, *review* what you learned by re-reading the list of main points. Also, for your easy preview, review, and reference, you'll find a master list of the collective main points from each chapter located at the back of this book.

✓ From this point in the book forward, the emphasis shifts from learning to develop a theoretical *view*, to the practical work of learning how to *do*. This is the next important step for you in developing *conscious competence* in the Transformational Daydreaming process.

✓ Since you have completed the *theoretical* Part I of this book and are now entering the *practice* phase, your key question needs to reflect this change. The overarching key question for the remainder of this book is, How can I use transformational daydreaming to help me _____ ?" From now on, when you have a concern, question, or problem that can benefit from the insights provided by the subconscious mind, you can ask this question and fill in the missing part with whatever your specific concern might be. For example: *how can I use transformational daydreaming to help me improve my physical health and wellness?*

✓ In this chapter, you explored step 1 of the 7-step Transformational Daydreaming program.

✓ You selected and named your Safe Place—somewhere where you feel safe, comfortable, and relaxed.

- ✓ To visit your Safe Place, all you need do is intend, close your eyes, repeat its name 3 times, and imagine being there feeling safe, comfortable, and relaxed.

- ✓ There are at least three main uses for your Safe Place; you can use your Safe Place to relax whenever you need to; you can use your Safe Place to contemplate and/or explore any of the more than 37 applications of daydreaming described in chapters 10; and you can use your Safe Place to communicate with the Subconscious Mind.

References

Rossman, M. (2000). *Guided imagery for self-healing.* Novato, CA: New World Library.

Storlie, T. (2015). *Person-centered communication with older adults.* San Diego, CA: Academic Press.

CHAPTER 6

STEP 2—RELAX AND ENTER AN ALTERED STATE

When you want to communicate with the subconscious, you use contemplation. When the subconscious mind wants to communicate with you, it uses spontaneous daydreams.

To enter an altered state, you need to feel safe, relaxed and comfortable. That's one of the main reasons you visit your Safe Place. Your objective at step 2 is simple. You want to trigger your body's automatic relaxation response—the body's natural tendency to feel safe, relaxed, and comfortable—and enter an altered state.

What is an Altered State?

You are a conscious, self-aware, human being. You sleep. You dream. You awaken. You daydream. These various states of awareness are considered normal and universal.

There are other states of awareness that can be triggered by meditation, hypnosis, enlightenment, panic, disease, starvation, dehydration, sleep deprivation, and pharmaceutical and plant substances. These are often labeled as *altered states of awareness.* Why altered?

Because being in a trance, uplifted in mystical rapture, suffering under the grip of disease, starvation, dehydration, or high on various drugs, is a different state of awareness from your routine, everyday state of wakeful awareness. It is an altered state.

Trance, Hypnosis, and Altered States of Awareness

It's important to clear up some common misconceptions about trance and altered states. Why? Because with accurate information and realistic expectations, you can easily go into an altered state and take full advantage of its many beneficial characteristics.

Television, movies, and other media, often portray hypnosis and trance in a distorted, sensationalistic, and exaggerated way. The truth is, hypnosis and trance are very common. Hypnosis is not about going to sleep. It's not about losing control. It's not about barking like a dog or developing amnesia. Contrary to the hype, hypnosis and trance are not at all glamorous.

> *Hypnosis and trance are common. Trance can make it easier for you to learn and see things differently.*

Alpha Brainwaves—All Hypnosis is Self-Hypnosis

When your eyes are closed for more than a couple of minutes, your brain shifts electrical activity and begins to increase production of alpha brain waves. Why is this important? Because that shift in the brain's electrical activity makes it easier for you to enter a state of awareness where the body can relax even more—where learning is often easier, deeper, and accelerated—and where you are more open to helpful, constructive suggestions. This altered state of awareness is viewed as a light hypnotic trance. In other words, trance can make it easier for you to learn and to begin to see things differently.

> *The truth is, all hypnosis is self-hypnosis.*
> *There is no other kind.*

Hypnosis is not a special, mystical, or strange state of mind. The altered state of awareness you'll experience in step 2, is a form of trance evoked by sitting physically relaxed, and mentally awake, aware, and with your eyes closed.

Trance is Very Common

Most people experience trance many times daily. It's likely you experience trance whenever you're contemplating something of deep interest, reading an engrossing novel, or watching an emotionally captivating TV program or movie. You experience trance whenever you are lost in thought, mentally wandering, or daydreaming. You probably experience trance while sitting and watching a bonfire, while listening to ghost stories, or whenever you "lose yourself" in a musical or artistic activity. Making love commonly induces a trance-like state as does relaxing in a hot tub.

When you are in lying in bed at night, preparing for sleep, eyes closed and feeling drowsy, not yet completely asleep and no longer fully awake, you are in a trance. You hover (for a brief time) in that middle area, that twilight state of neither awake, nor asleep.

Many common experiences of daily living also can induce an altered state—a trance. Here's one example: you're driving your car on a long journey. You still have many, monotonous miles to go before you arrive at your destination. Maybe you're feeling bored or sleepy. All of a sudden, you become aware you've driven many more miles than you thought. You wonder, "where did the miles go?" The truth is you experienced a mild form of "highway hypnosis" and time distortion. It was like you were driving on auto-pilot. You were not asleep, but your mind wandered off down memory lane while another part of you (the subconscious mind) knew exactly what to do to continue safely operating your vehicle.

As you can see from the examples above, you experience trance daily. Within the transformational daydreaming process, you'll go into a trance like you've done so many times before, but with one important difference. In the examples provided above, you went into a trance—an altered state—and then you came out of it, back into your normal, routine state of awareness without *using* the trance. You experienced the trance but did not take advantage of the trance. Here, you'll enter into trance and while in this altered state of awareness, you'll purposefully take advantage of the enhanced learning capability and increased openness to constructive suggestions associated with this state of mind.

You are already very experienced and skilled at going into a light trance. Now you can do it knowledgeably and at will, to help enhance your personal and/or professional life. The following section explains one easy method you can use to enter a trance-like altered state of awareness.

Countdown to Relaxation Method

There are dozens of ways to trigger your body's relaxation response and enter an altered state. One method is called *Countdown to Relaxation*. This method is easy and effective. It is commonly used (in some form and under various names) by professionals who use hypnosis and/or teach relaxation techniques. This method, is based on easy-to-learn techniques that help trigger your relaxation response.

It's one I developed several years ago for a group of hospice professionals attending an all-day workshop I conducted on stress management.

Instructions

- Sit with your eyes gently closed and unfocused. There should be no strain around your eyes or forehead. Use your imagination and go to your Safe Place.

- Relax for a few minutes and then mentally suggest to yourself, *"As I mentally count down from 7 to 1, I feel more and more relaxed and begin to enter an altered state of awareness."* That's what you want to be thinking when you are counting down. Make sure you use a mental voice (the voice in your head) that's soft, slow, and soothing. Count the numbers with a voice that expresses the tone and the tempo you would use if you were trying to help someone else relax—soothing, comforting.

- Begin to mentally count down from 7 to 1. Notice that with each decreasing number, you begin to feel more safe, relaxed, and comfortable. Take one easy, natural breath with each number you count, starting with the number 7. With each inhalation, think or visualize the number. With each exhalation, think the phrase *"safe, relaxed, comfortable."* For example: inhale and imagine the number 7. Exhale and think the words, *"safe, relaxed, comfortable."*

- After reaching the number 1, deepen your relaxation even more. Vividly recall a specific relaxing memory—a time and/or a situation when you really felt relaxed. Recall this memory for another 10 or 15 seconds. When you feel deeply relaxed, mentally repeat, *"I feel safe, relaxed, and comfortable."* After much practice and repetition, just thinking these words often trigger the associated feelings.

- Deepen your altered state. With your hands in your lap, gently touch the tip of each index finger to the tip of each thumb (see illustration below). This hand position is called a *mudra*. Mudras have been in common use for thousands of years in India and elsewhere. This particular mudra is believed to help you relax, focus, and it supports entering an altered state of consciousness. Mentally suggest to yourself that you will deepen your altered state simply by counting down from 3 to 1 and at the number 1, you'll be in a deep, altered state.

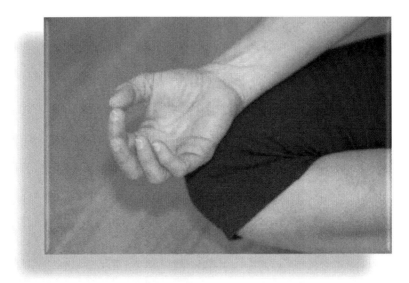

- You are still in your Safe Place. With eyes closed and without moving your head, let your eyes shift slightly to the right side and see the number 3 there. It's your imagination, you can see it however you choose. With your attention still focused on the right side, slowly, mentally count "3, 3, 3." Without moving your head, shift your eyes to the middle of your visual field — as if you're looking straight ahead but with your eyes still closed — and see the number 2 there. With your attention in the middle, slowly, mentally count "2, 2, 2." And now, without moving your head, shift your eyes to the left side of your visual field and see the number 1. With your attention on the left side, slowly mentally count *"1, 1, 1."* Now, just rest your eyes and relax in a deeply altered state. [note: when doing the complete 7-step transformational daydreaming process, this is the point that you would begin contemplation]

- When you're ready to be done, suggest to yourself that in the next few seconds of clock time, you're going to open your eyes, feel wide awake, relaxed, and in your normal, everyday state of awareness—able to go about your activities awake, alert, and safe. Do it.

Please read over these instructions several times. Try reading them aloud too. Remember, repetition aids learning. It takes most people 10-20 times or more of practice before they are able to complete this procedure from memory. Do not feel intimidated by the number of words it took to explain this. Use the techniques of deliberate, deep practice. First, get the "big picture." Then break the big picture into its smaller component parts. Learn each component part and then put them all back together. Others have done this. You can do it too!

A Commonly Asked Question

Q: Is it really necessary to use the Safe Place—to go to all the trouble of remembering or imagining some place where we feel safe, relaxed, and comfortable?

A: Yes! Why? Because working from within your Safe Place provides you with many benefits—benefits that you will grow to appreciate as time passes. Working in your Safe Place helps you physically and emotionally relax. It helps to develop your imagery and contemplation skills. And, it helps you shift the brain's electrical activity so you can quickly enter an altered state. With regular use over time, simply going to your Safe Place can evoke the ideal state of mind for you to enjoy communication with your subconscious mind. And, the self-hypnosis process you're learning can be used for any constructive, worthwhile purpose.

Conclusion

In this chapter, you learned step 2 of the 7-step transformational daydreaming system—how to use the countdown to relaxation method and enter and deepen your altered state.

In the next chapter, you'll learn all about contemplation—step 3. Because this is such an important skill for communicating with the subconscious mind, please proceed mindfully, thoroughly, and patiently. Why not do whatever is required to really master the art of contemplation? You'll be glad you did!

List of Main Points for Preview and Review

- ✓ Begin each chapter by first turning to the end of the chapter so you can *preview* the list of main points. After completing your preview, then carefully *read* the chapter and complete each exercise. Finally, *review* what you learned by re-reading the list of main points. Also, for your easy preview, review, and reference, you'll find a master list of the collective main points from each chapter located at the back of this book.

- ✓ From this point in the book forward, the emphasis shifts from learning to develop a theoretical *view*, to the practical work of learning how to *do*. This is the next important step for you in developing *conscious competence* in the Transformational Daydreaming process.

- ✓ Since you have completed the *theoretical* Part I of this book and are now entering the *practice* phase, your key question needs to reflect this change. The overarching key question for the remainder of this book is, *How can I use transformational daydreaming to help me _____?"* From now on, when you have a concern, question, or problem that can benefit from the insights provided by the subconscious mind, you can ask this question and fill in the missing part with whatever your specific concern might be. For example: *how can I use transformational daydreaming to help me improve my physical health and wellness?*

- ✓ Whatever issue you face—whether it's physical, emotional, social, financial, mental, personal, professional, religious, psychic, transpersonal, or spiritual—you can use the same empowering question to orient your view and thought process in a solution-focused manner. Using the transformational daydreaming process, the focus is on *doing*. What can you *do* about your concern?

- ✓ In this chapter, you explored step 2 of the 7-step Transformational Daydreaming program.

- ✓ In step two, you learned to enter an altered state of awareness (or trance) using the Countdown to Relaxation Method, self-suggestion, and a special hand position called a *mudra.*

References

Baruss, I. (2003). *Alterations of consciousness: An empirical analysis for social scientists*. Washington, D.C.: American Psychological Association.

Freeman, L.W., & Lawlis, G.F. (2001). *Mosby's complementary an alternative medicine: A research-based approach*. St. Louis, MO: Mosby.

Fries, A. (2009). *Daydreams at work: Wake up your creative powers*. Sterling, VA: Capital Books.

Gale Reference Team. (2001). Daydreaming. Gale Encyclopedia of Psychology.

Klinger, E. (1990). *Daydreaming: Using waking fantasy and imagery for self-knowledge and creativity*. Los Angeles, CA: Tarcher.

Rao, R.K. (2002). *Consciousness Studies: Cross-cultural perspectives*. Jefferson, NC: McFarland & Co.

Rossman, M. (2000). *Guided imagery for self-healing*. Novato, CA: New World Library.

Singer, J. (2009). Researching imaginative play and adult consciousness: Implications for daily and literary creativity. Psychology of Aesthetics, Creativity, and the Arts 3(4), 190-199.

Smallwood, J., Beach, E., Schooler, J.W., & Handy, T.C. (2008). Going AWOL in the brain: Mind wandering reduces cortical analysis of external events. Journal of Cognitive Neuroscience 20(3), 458-469.

CHAPTER 7

STEP 3—CONTEMPLATE TO COMMUNICATE WITH YOUR SUBCONSCIOUS MIND

In this Chapter

In the previous chapter, you learned to enter an altered state after going to your Safe Place to relax. In this chapter, you'll complete the third step and learn advanced contemplation—a core technique used primarily to initiate communication with your subconscious mind.

> *When you want to communicate with the subconscious, you use contemplation. When the subconscious mind wants to communicate with you, it uses spontaneous daydreams.*

The Key Question—a Tool You can use for the Rest of Your Life

Each chapter includes plenty of planned repetition and the following suggestions for accelerating your learning, increasing comprehension and retention, and getting the most from this book. As you study this chapter, be sure and read with the *new* key question in mind. The new key question is,

"How can I use transformational daydreaming to help me _____ ?"

The final part of the key question has been purposefully left blank. You can complete the question with whatever words best address your present concern. For example: *how can I use transformational daydreaming to help me improve my contemplation skills?*

This new key question can help orient your view and nudge your thought process in a solution-focused direction. This helps you focus on *doing*—on taking action. What can you *do* about your concern? In this example, what can you *do* to improve your contemplative skills?

> *The key question is a tool you can use for the rest of your life to help you create a better life — the life you hope for.*

With your new key question in mind, turn to the end of this chapter and *preview* the list of main points. After completing your preview, begin to carefully *read* the chapter. Make sure you complete each exercise. Finally, turn back to the end of this chapter and *review* the list of main points.

This recipe for deep learning, if faithfully followed, will help maximize your learning experience.

What is Contemplation?

Contemplation is deep, relaxed, reflective thought about something that absorbs your attention. Although contemplation is most often done with your eyes closed, it is possible to contemplate with eyes open.

Other terms used for contemplation include: *pondering, mulling things over,* and *musing*. Although contemplation is a popular stand-alone technique, within the transformational daydreaming system, it is used primarily as a means of communication with the subconscious mind.

> *Contemplation is relaxed, deep, meditative, reflective thought.*

Before diving deeper into the topic of contemplation, there are a few important terms and concepts that first need to be reviewed. Understanding these concepts will increase the clarity, power, and effectiveness of your use of multi-sensory mental imagery.

Multi-Sensory Imagery—Language of the Subconscious Mind

The concept of *multi-sensory imagery*, refers to a specific type of visualization. Multi-sensory imagery or visualization uses memories, imagination, inner vision, sounds, touch, tastes, and smells.

You might feel a little confused by the word *imagery* because it tends to imply exclusively visual. But in this context, it is truly multi-sensorial and used interchangeably with the term *visualization* (Bone & Ellen,1992). The key point is that within this system, multi-sensory imagery is viewed as the language of the subconscious mind.

The Importance of Physical and Emotional Realism

Convincing physiological evidence exists to support the effectiveness of using tactical imagery. Sophisticated brain scans and near-infrared spectroscopy measurements show that during mental imaging, many of the same parts of the brain are activated that would be if the actions were being physically completed.

Siddle (2008) described how when athletes attached to biofeedback instruments imagined performing a specific skill, electrical signals were detected in the same muscle groups that would be involved if the skill was being physically executed. He also demonstrated that when a specific skill is visualized, a measurable increase of blood flow to that area of the body was observed.

When you work with contemplative mental imagery, it's important to focus on *realism*. Your imagery should be as realistic as possible (Asken, Grossman, & Christensen, 2010). The representative images of specific people, places, events, and associated feelings used within your contemplation, should accurately reflect their related physical counterparts. Your imagery should accurately reflect the physical environment or situation related to your contemplation.

Realistic imagery also includes visualizing events in real-time speed and experiencing emotions that you'd be feeling if events related to your contemplation were physically occurring (Siddle, 2008).

Active Intentional Imagery, Receptive Spontaneous Imagery, End-State Imagery, and Process Imagery

While contemplating, you often use four primary types of imagery: *active imagery, receptive imagery, process imagery,* and *end-state imagery.*

1. *Active imagery* is imagery you produce intentionally—it's something you do purposefully (Achterberg, Dossey, & Kolkmeier, 1994). You decide to do it, you do it, and you know you're doing it. Active imagery plays an important role in contemplation.

    For example, intentionally imagine that you sit down, close your eyes, and go to your Safe Place. That is an example of using active imagery.

2. *Receptive imagery* is spontaneous and automatic. It is unplanned—something unintentional that comes from "out of the blue" (Achterberg, Dossey, & Kolkmeier, 1994). You don't decide to do it. It just happens and you notice it. Receptive imagery is spontaneous daydreaming and originates from the subconscious.

    For example, imagine you sit down, close your eyes, and go to your Safe Place. You begin to witness a spontaneous stream of images, sounds, and feelings. Relaxing deeply, you drift along a path of seemingly unrelated memories. After a few minutes, you become aware you've been thinking of an old high-school sweetheart. You didn't intend to recall this historical experience, it "just happened." This is receptive, spontaneous imagery—communication from the subconscious mind.

3. *Process imagery.* In addition to active intentional and receptive spontaneous imagery, imagery is either *process*

imagery or *end-state imagery* (Achterberg, Dossey, & Kolkmeier, 1994). Process imagery is step-by-step and sequential. It's critical in the learning of skills that require serial or sequential steps. Process imagery reveals how to get from point A to point Z by traveling through points B, C, D, etc. It reveals how to get to your desired destination. It's much like following GPS instructions or a road map.

Process imagery can be compared to a recipe that explains what to do first, then second and so on, until your dish is fully prepared. Additional examples abound such as putting together your child's bike, assembling a bookcase, changing a flat tire on a car, writing a book, learning a sport such as martial arts, learning a new dance routine, traveling to a distant destination, or how to play musical instruments such as a guitar or piano.

4. *End-state imagery* is visualizing the task or final outcome as if it's already completed (Achterberg, Dossey, & Kolkmeier, 1994). For example, instead of seeing yourself preparing a meal (as in process imagery), you see the meal already prepared (end-state imagery).

Instead of imagining writing a book (process imagery), imagine your book is already finished and you are handing it to your publisher (end-state imagery). Again, examples abound: you visualize the bike already assembled, the bookcase assembled; the flat tire on the car changed, having arrived at your destination, playing a favorite song on your guitar or piano.

Multi-Sensory Imagery

When you sit down to contemplate—to ask the subconscious mind for an insightful, informative daydream—you want to combine the many types of imagery—intentional, spontaneous, process, and end-state. Your imagery should be realistic. It should involve as many senses as possible—seeing, hearing, smelling, feeling, and sensing. You want to use process imagery for visualizing the steps from start to finish, and end-state imagery for visualizing the final objective as if it's already complete.

Self-Talk

Contemplation also involves mental self-talk. For best results, your self-talk should be present focused and include both process-oriented language and end-state language. For example, if you were imagining traveling to Hawaii, your self-talk might sound like this: *"I am boarding the plane for Hawaii"* (this is one of many steps required to get you from where you are to where you want to be—Hawaii). And then, *"I am standing on a beautiful Hawaiian beach."* That's end-state self-talk (a statement related to the achievement of your goal—to be in Hawaii). Please make sure you're clear on the difference between process oriented self-talk and end-state oriented self-talk.

You may find exposure to these new terms and definitions a bit confusing, but understanding these concepts—and your ability to integrate them into your mental imagery—will significantly increase the clarity, power, and effectiveness of your work. The effort you make to understand these terms and use the concepts will be worth it. There's one more concept you need to understand. And it has some very practical, eyes-open applications as you will learn.

Forward and Backward Chaining

A task has a beginning, middle, and end. This view of task completion starts with step one and progresses sequentially, step after step until completion. You progress from the beginning to the end.

This is called *forward chaining*. Forward chaining is commonly used for tasks requiring directions for completion. Forward chaining is often used in a *how-to* strategy—how to assemble your child's new bike.

Sometimes it's helpful (or necessary) to imagine task completion in reverse order—beginning at the end (the final step) and working backward to the beginning (the first step). You progress from the end to the beginning. This is called *backward chaining*.

Backward chaining is commonly used to help accelerate learning and deepen memorization. Backward chaining is a *deep practice* strategy. Depending on your contemplation topic you might want to use one or both.

As a helpful aside, here's a practical technique that can help you remember where you parked your car when you're out shopping, eating, seeing a movie, or attending an event. It incorporates both forward and backward chaining and provides a good example of how each is used with eyes-open contemplation.

Technique: Where's My Car?

Has this ever happened to you?

1. You go to a store to do some shopping.
2. You arrive at the parking lot. It's nearly full. You circle around and finally find a parking spot.
3. You park your car, get out, lock it up, and then walk into the store thinking about what you need and where it can be found.
4. You finish your shopping, come out the door, and then stand there looking out over the sea of cars thinking, "oh crap! Where's my car?"

Look at this familiar scene below. It shows a woman—standing in a parking lot, surrounded by a sea of cars—trying to remember where she parked her car.

Transformational Daydreaming

Forgetting where you parked your car is a common experience. Why? Because many people do not allow enough time, or pay close enough attention to detail, to move the memory of where their car is parked from working-memory to short-term memory. Here's a technique I've used for years to eliminate this embarrassing problem. Trust me, when you use this technique, it will be much easier to remember where you parked your car. Next time you go shopping, try this:

1. Park your car, get out and lock the doors.

2. Before moving away from your car toward the store, stand next to your car for about 10-15 seconds. During this short time, look at your car and then glance around and notice what's near your car—landmarks, a tree, the spot people return their shopping carts, a fire hydrant. It could be anything. Now, look back at your car. Repeat this back-and-forth looking a few times. Look at a landmark and then back at your car. This helps your brain associate the location of your car with what is near it.

3. Continue standing next to your car for a few more

seconds. Imagine yourself quickly walking to the door of the store. Stop, turn around and look back to where your car is parked. See it parked next to those things near it. See yourself walking directly back to your car. Repeat this visualization 2-3 times in rapid succession. It appears like a speeded-up movie where you see yourself walking from your car to the door of the store and then from the door of the store, back to your car. Forward to the door of the store and backward from the store to your car. This is an example of forward and backward chaining that greatly improves memory.

4. Now, stop your visualization and physically walk to the door of the store. Just before you physically enter the store, pause, turn around and take notice of where your car is parked and what is nearby.

If this technique works as well for you as it does for me, then you should no longer have any trouble recalling where you parked your car.

Transformational Daydreaming: Step 3 — Contemplate to Communicate with Your Subconscious Mind

Your theoretical preparation is complete. The pieces are in place. It's time to begin your practice of contemplation. This is step 3 of the 7-step process. This could be one of the most beneficial practices you will ever learn. That will be up to you.

Whenever you decide to contemplate, you first select a topic upon which to contemplate. For example, you want to improve your ability to communicate with your subconscious mind. That's your topic for contemplation in this example.

Here's one way to do it:

1. Go to your Safe Place, relax, and enter an altered state —

just like you were taught in steps 1 and 2 of the 7-step process.

2. Resting in your Safe Place, alert, awake and in an altered state, begin to gently focus your attention on your topic of contemplation. Contemplate in a relaxed, curious frame of mind. No tension, no rush. No hurry, no worry. Stay relaxed and curious. The goal is to contemplate and eventually communicate with your subconscious mind, not just see how many different techniques you can use.

3. Think about the overall "big picture"—the outcome you desire. Mentally walk around that end-state imagery where you are successfully communicating with the subconscious mind. What does that look like? What do you see and sense that lets you know you have been successful? What does that successful outcome look, sound, and feel like to you? It might feel inspiring to see yourself able to communicate with your subconscious mind.

While contemplating on this topic, make sure to use everything you learned that might enhance the clarity of your message. This does not mean you should use *every* technique you learned. No. It means you should make your message as clear as you possibly can, given you are communicating with images and feelings not words. Depending on your intended message, this may include multi-sensory imagery, process and end-state imagery, and receptive and active imagery. If appropriate, use forward and backward chaining. If needed, use process-oriented self-talk and end-state oriented self-talk.

> *The key is to use whatever you believe enhances the clarity and meaning of your "message" to the your subconscious mind.*

Think about it. Mull it over. This is contemplation. The goal is to create a clear, concise, contemplative message that accurately communicates your desire. Just enough, no more, no less. Here's an example of contemplation that someone shared.

Topic of Contemplation: *"I want to improve my daily diet and eat higher-quality, more nutritious, home-cooked meals."*

Contemplation: Sitting at my dining room table, I'm eating a meal that I prepared. It's a delicious, highly-nutritious, home-cooked meal. The food smells wonderful and tastes even better! The warm food feels good in my tummy. I thoroughly enjoy my meal and feel proud of myself. [note: this is multi-sensorial and end-state imagery]

I am standing in the kitchen browsing through my cookbooks. I select a recipe that looks easy to prepare yet is healthy and delicious. I make a list of all the ingredients I need to prepare this dish. [note: this is forward-chaining, realistic, and process imagery]

I'm at the grocery store walking around the fruits and vegetable section looking over all the fresh, organic food selections. I easily locate all the ingredients on my list and purchase them. As I walk out of the store, I feel good about myself for making the food purchases. [note: this is forward-chaining, realistic, and process imagery]

I am standing in my kitchen. All the ingredients, spices, bowls, plates, knives, and cooking utensils needed are arranged on the counter. I wash my hands and hum a pleasant song I heard on the radio today. I feel good. I carefully follow each step of the recipe. Soon, the healthy, nutritious, and delicious meal is complete and ready to eat. It smells so good! I notice my mouth is watering! [note: this is forward-chaining, realistic, and process imagery]

I'm sitting at the dining room table. I feel relaxed and ready to enjoy a wonderful meal. I begin to eat. Everything smells go enticing and tastes so delicious! I feel good knowing the food I am eating not only is a real taste sensation, but is healthy and good for me. [note: this is forward-chaining, realistic, and process imagery]

I am wrapping up some left-overs and placing them in the refrigerator. The aroma of good food lingers in the air and my stomach feels pleasantly satisfied. I feel proud of myself for taking the time to prepare such a wonderful meal. Talking out loud to myself, I say, "I want to prepare these kinds of home-cooked, healthy, delicious meals several times each week." I smile and nod my head slowly up and down in a yes-like motion.

4. Imagine you are the subconscious mind and have just received the above message. Does the contemplation deliver the message? Is it clear what you are asking for or asking about? Does it convey what you want? If not, revise it until it does.

[Note: if this were not a practice exercise and you were doing the entire transformational daydreaming process, this is the point where you would stop active contemplation. You would cease contemplation and sit in quiet, receptive, expectancy—patiently waiting for a

response from your subconscious mind. See the final section below for more information.]

5. When your contemplation feels complete, follow the steps you learned to come out of an altered state, awaken yourself, and mentally leave your Safe Place. Be fully awake physically and fully alert mentally. Open your eyes and record a brief summary of your contemplative experience focusing on your thoughts and feelings. Here's an important tip. Assume everything that happened during your contemplation was related to your stated concern. Honor your experience by thinking about it, paying attention to it, and writing it down.

Your Unique Contemplations

Your contemplative experience is unique. It may sometimes surprise you. It might sometimes disappoint you. It will almost certainly be different than you expected. This is what you can expect—that there is little you can expect. What happens is what happens. Your contemplation may be mostly visual. It might be mainly auditory. It could be more kinesthetic or emotional. Or it could be you simply have a general awareness of things. Your contemplations could be a mix of all the above. The point is, experiences differ from person to person and even from session to session. There's really no one right way, there's just the way that's right for you. Keep an open-mind and pay attention to what happens.

Remember, contemplation is a skill. The time, practice, and efforts you invest now to master its usage will pay huge future dividends. Why? Because you'll be able to use contemplation to help improve all areas of your personal and/or professional life—for the rest of your life.

Difference Between Practice of Contemplation by Itself and Practice of Contemplation as part of the Entire 7-Step System

The contemplation exercise above provided an example of using contemplation as a stand-alone technique. When contemplation is used as part of the entire transformational daydreaming process, there is one important difference.

In the contemplation exercise, when you finished step 5, you stopped and began the process of reawakening and reorientation in step 6. When using the full 7-step process, when you complete step 5—instead of reawaking and reorienting yourself—you'll sit in a quiet, expectant, and receptive state of mind and patiently wait for the subconscious to respond with a spontaneous daydream. You are not doing that here but it's coming very soon, so please be patient.

At this point in your development, you are still assembling the 7-step system piece by piece. You are connecting the steps in a forward chain and you're almost there!

Why would you settle for mediocrity when mastery is available?

Question and Answer

Q: Please re-explain the goal of contemplation.

A: In general, artists, mystics, philosophers, scientists, writers, and many others, often use contemplation as part of their creative process.

In transformational daydreaming, the goal of contemplation is for you to be able to communicate your intent to the subconscious mind. You're talking with the subconscious mind using the language that it understands—multi-sensory symbolic imagery. When it's time for you to be quiet and listen, what you're looking and listening for, is a response from the subconscious mind in the form of a spontaneous daydream. Make sense?

Conclusion

In this chapter, you learned how to contemplate. For your ease of reference, the entire process is repeated in the *List of Main Points for Preview and Review* section that follows. This will make it easy to use when practicing. Contemplation is the focus of step 3 of the 7-step Transformational Daydreaming process. In the next chapter, you'll learn the 4 remaining steps.

List of Main Points for Preview and Review

* Practice Copy – How to Contemplate *

- ✓ Select your topic for contemplation. For example, "I want to improve communication with the subconscious mind." Relax, enter an altered state, and go to your Safe Place (steps 1-2).

- ✓ Resting in your Safe Place, begin by loosely focusing attention on your topic for a couple of minutes. Think about your desired final outcome (end-state). What do you want? What does a successful outcome look, sound, and feel like?

- ✓ Use active imagery. Consciously think about it. Mull it over. Mentally look at it from various viewpoints—through your eyes, through the eyes of another. Ponder. Wonder. Let your thoughts percolate on the subject. Explore possible connections between the concept of your topic and other concepts. What does it remind you of?

- ✓ Remember, your contemplation is a message you are sending to the subconscious mind. You are using an image language rather than a word-based language. Focus on making your message clear. Use all the tricks—the "secret language" (multi-sensory imagery), process-imagery, end-state imagery, receptive and active imagery, multiple points of view, forward and backward chaining, self-talk, emotions, real-time, imagining an actual environment—whatever helps to clearly convey your request.

- ✓ In your contemplation, use step-by-step, process-imagery to show how the outcome is being achieved and end-state imagery that depicts a successful outcome. Experience it as if it's actually happening. Make it real. You need to communicate how you feel about whatever it is you are requesting from the subconscious mind. [note: review the example of meal preparation used in *Exercise 3*]

✓ Do all this in a relaxed, curious frame of mind.

✓ When done, mentally exit your Safe Place, consciously come back to where you are now. Be fully alert. Return to your normal wakeful awareness and open your eyes.

✓ Record a brief summary of your contemplative experience focusing on your thoughts and emotions. Assume everything that happened during your contemplation was related to your stated intention or was part of an answer to a question asked. Honor whatever your experience was by paying attention to it and writing it down.

✓ Remember, your experience may be different than expected. Some people contemplate primarily visually. Others are more auditory, kinesthetic, or simply seem to have a general sense of things.

✓ Experiences differ from person to person and even from session to session. There is no one right way. There is only your way.

✓ There is a difference between using contemplation as a stand-alone technique and using it as part of the entire 7-step process.

✓ Master contemplation. It's a skill you can use to improve nearly all aspects of your life, for the rest of your life.

References

Achterberg, J., & Dossey, B., Kolkmeier, L. (1994). *Rituals of healing: Using imagery for health and wellness.* New York: NY: Bantam Books.

Baruss, I. (2003). *Alterations of consciousness: An empirical analysis for social scientists.* Washington, D.C.: American Psychological Association.

Bone, P.F., & Ellen, P.S. (1992). The generation and consequences of communication-evoked imagery. *Journal of Consumer Research, 19,* 93-104.

Freeman, L.W., & Lawlis, G.F. (2001). *Mosby's complementary and alternative medicine: A research-based approach.* St. Louis, MO: Mosby.

Fries, A. (2009). *Daydreams at work: Wake up your creative powers.* Sterling, VA: Capital Books.

Gale Reference Team. (2001). Daydreaming. *Gale Encyclopedia of Psychology.*

Klinger, E. (1990). *Daydreaming: Using waking fantasy and imagery for self-knowledge and creativity.* Los Angeles: Tarcher.

Morris, T., Spittle, M., and Watt, A. (2005). *Imagery in sport.* Champaign, ILL: Human Kinetics.

Rao, R.K. (2002). *Consciousness Studies: Cross-cultural perspectives.* Jefferson, NC: McFarland & Co.

Siddle, B.K. (2008). *Sharpening the warrior's edge: The psychology of science and training.* Belleville, IL: PPCT Research Publications.

Singer, J. (2009). Researching imaginative play and adult consciousness: Implications for daily and literary creativity. Psychology of Aesthetics, Creativity, and the Arts 3(4), 190-199.

Smallwood, J., Beach, E., Schooler, J.W., & Handy, T.C. (2008). Going AWOL in the brain: Mind wandering reduces cortical analysis of external events. Journal of Cognitive Neuroscience 20(3), 4.

CHAPTER 8

STEPS 4-7

"When you want to communicate with the subconscious, you use contemplation. When the subconscious mind wants to communicate with you, it uses spontaneous daydreams."

In this Chapter

In the previous chapters, you were introduced to steps 1, 2, and 3 of the 7-step Transformational Daydreaming communication process. In this chapter, you'll learn the 4 remaining steps. For your reference, here are the 7 steps:

1. Go to your Safe Place.
2. Relax and enter an altered state.
3. Contemplate to communicate with your subconscious mind. *This is how you ask for help.*
4. Receive a daydream from your subconscious mind. *This is how you receive help.*
5. Return to normal wakeful awareness.
6. Exit your Safe Place.
7. Document, analyze, and interpret daydream.

Once you study, learn, and practice all 7 steps, you'll be able to explore and experiment with more than 37 different applications for communicating with your super-intelligence within. These and other applications are explored in chapter 10. As you study this chapter, be sure to read with the *new* key question in mind.

"How can I use transformational daydreaming to help me _____ ?"

Quick Review of Steps 1-3 in Preparation for Moving to Step 4

In step 1, *Go to Your Safe Place*—the place where you feel safe, relaxed, and comfortable.

In step 2, *Relax and Enter an Altered State* using the *Countdown to Relaxation* method.

In step 3, *Contemplation to Communicate with Your Subconscious Mind,* you asked your subconscious mind to listen to your concerns. You then presented your concerns to the subconscious mind via your multi-sensory contemplation.

In step 4, *Receive a Daydream*, you are attempting to consciously receive communication from the subconscious mind—that part of you believed to be at least 1 million times more powerful than you, as the conscious personality.

Step 4 – Receive a Daydream

Stop consciously contemplating. Patiently, passively, and receptively sit, wait, and pay attention. Wait for the subconscious to respond. Watch. Listen. Sit with a curious attitude of detached expectancy and remain open to what happens next. Pay close attention to any details you become aware of—small or large, mundane or marvelous.

Allow the subconscious mind complete freedom and autonomy to direct the daydreaming process with absolutely no conscious interference from you. This communication process has little chance of success unless you're willing to take your conscious hands off the steering wheel and allow the subconscious mind to show up when it's good and ready to take its place in the driver's seat, and drive the bus free of your judgment and micromanagement. The more you are present as a conscious directing influence, the less present will be the subconscious mind.

> *The more you are present as a conscious directing influence, the less present will be the subconscious mind.*

Remaining open and passive and yet with expectancy as you watch and listen, allow any daydreaming activity to unfold spontaneously. Be receptive to what occurs. Remember, the response from the subconscious mind could be anything from nothing at all, to a glimpse of faint and confusing images; a mixed grab bag of personal memories; barely audible words or sounds; subtle impressions, sensations, or feelings; and any and all combinations of these experiences, all the way to the experience of a full mental movie.

When step 4 feels complete, or you've had enough, you will begin to shift to ending your daydream with steps 5 and 6. But before that, here is some important information about this shift from contemplation to daydreaming.

The Shift from Contemplation to Spontaneous Daydreaming

There are many ways you might experience this shift. Some are vague and subtle, some clear and stark. Below is an example of how it feels to shift from step 3 (contemplation) to step 4 (daydreaming).

A typical experience might go something like this. Sitting with your eyes closed in your Safe Place, you feel relaxed and in an altered state. You have a specific question, concern, or desire. You've asked the subconscious mind for help, and now, you're consciously contemplating on your desire.

During contemplation, there are moments when your mind seems to wander. You become aware you're not contemplating in the same way you were a moment ago—that you're thinking about something completely different. It's as if you catch yourself contemplating upon an unrelated topic. You catch a glimpse of images or maybe the hint of a sound that you didn't purposely choose, and you didn't consciously imagine. As you become more relaxed and drift into a deeper altered state, these momentary lapses often increase. They could even develop into a completely spontaneous daydream. If this occurs, your detached observation is a must.

Why? Because some people get excited at this point, and guess what? The curtain closes. They lose awareness of the daydream. Why? Too much conscious mind is present. This is exactly the point where detached curiosity is important.

It's as if the excitement shifted control away from the subconscious mind back to the conscious mind—just the opposite of what you're trying to do.

As you gain experience, your ability to let go and allow the subconscious mind free reign will improve. It takes much practice. Progress is rarely linear, rarely in a straight line. It's more realistic to expect a zig-zag journey full of unexpected twists and turns. Knowing this ahead of time will help you avoid disappointment or worse still, blaming yourself for "not doing it right." Learn from your experience. Keep trying.

There is no failure, but there is feedback. Pay close attention to your experience. Learn from it.

People sometimes fall asleep and experience an actual sleeping dream. Although that's not your goal, it's okay and you might even experience a dream related to your question or concern. If you fall asleep, it probably just means you're relaxed and maybe a little tired. But do your best to follow the system.

At first you may experience virtually no spontaneous daydreams. Again, that's okay, because with practice, you'll most likely begin experiencing these glimpses—these momentary lapses mentioned. You could even experience the holy grail of daydream experiences—the full, spontaneous, and lucid daydream.

Step 5 – Be Awake and Alert

The daydream feels complete or you have decided to conclude your session for other reasons. What do you do? You thank the subconscious mind and begin the process of returning to your ordinary state of awareness.

Remind yourself you can return to your Safe Place anytime you want by simply intending to, closing your eyes, and mentally repeating the name of your Safe Place three times.

Step 6 – Exit Your Safe Place

Suggest to yourself that when you open your eyes, you will feel awake, alert, fully conscious, and with excellent recall of whatever you may have experienced. Gently open your eyes, bringing all of your experiences, learnings, insights, and "aha's" with you.

Step 7- Document and Analyze Your Daydream

Stop! Do not engage in any other activity until you complete this final step. Why? Because your daydreams are much like your night dreams. They are easily forgotten and can quickly evaporate in the presence of competing thoughts.

What's the point of completing this 7-step process for communicating with your subconscious mind if afterword you can't recall the advice given?

To improve your daydream recall, the most helpful task you can do is to write it down immediately after you finish your session. The physical act of writing it down helps cement it into your memory and demonstrates that you value the information shared.

Write down only what you can specifically recall of your daydream experience, even if it seems random and unrelated. This is not the time for guesswork, speculation, or interpretation. That will come later. Like the dreams of the night, the dreams of the day are symbolic (Barth, 1997).

What did you experience specifically? Remembering a daydream can range from a glimpse of vague images, feelings, sensations, sounds, smells, to fleeting personal memories, or a mental movie.

As you record your daydream, regard everything you experienced as potentially useful information. Assume all aspects of your daydream were symbolically related to your stated concern. Write everything you can recall down on paper before proceeding.

When you have recorded as much as you can honestly recall, then ask yourself if you believe your subconscious responded to your request for help. If you feel it did, what specifically makes you believe your subconscious responded to your request for help? Again, write down only what you experienced. Just the facts as you recall them. Do not guess, speculate, or interpret at this point. Simply describe your actual experience. As an example, here are some notes from my daydream journal: "I felt a warm feeling in my abdominal area. Then, I was sitting on the bank next to a creek. I looked at the water flowing by me. I realized I am not the stream of flowing water. I am separate from the water—the observer of the water."

If you believe you had a genuine response from the subconscious mind, then the next most important question you can ask is, "What is this daydream trying to tell me?" (Feinstein & Krippner, 2006). Reflect on your daydream in its entirety. Try to capture the holistic essence of the message by summarizing what you can recall in a single phrase or sentence. Again, ask, "What is this daydream trying to tell me?"

What comes to you? How does the daydream make you feel? What does it remind you of? Did this daydream provide you with any immediate and obvious insight into your concern? If so, describe it with as much detail as you feel is helpful. What was your subconscious trying to tell you?

What is the single most important insight this response is trying to communicate to you? For example, in a previous paragraph above, I shared an excerpt from my daydream journal. This daydream was in response to my question asking how I could deepen my meditations. My analysis suggested I sit as a detached observer and simply watch the passing stream of thoughts as they flow by. My interpretation was that I am not my thoughts, I am pure awareness.

A note of caution, especially if you receive a lot of information from your daydream. You want to lean toward information that is new and novel. When reflecting upon your daydream—in its entirety or in its parts—you will often experience an "aha." Taylor, (2009) describes the "aha" recognition as a trustworthy guide to discovering authentic, accurate interpretations but cautions that the initial "aha" moments are likely to occur over things you already know or recognize.

The treasure lies in the sense of surprise—the "aha" that takes you beyond what you already know. Delaney (1996) agrees. She writes, "You will know that you have succeeded in interpreting your dream when it tells you something you did not realize before." After all, why would your subconscious mind waste time communicating something you already think you know? Be cautious of responses that only seem to confirm what you already know, believe, or suspect. Pay particular attention to whatever information challenges your current beliefs, prejudices, and understandings.

Next, look at the individual parts and symbols of the daydream. List the people, places, activities, images, sounds, sensations, and emotions you observed. What feelings do you have about each of these images? What words or ideas come to mind when you recall this image? Do you feel energized by this image? Does this image remind you of anything that is connected to your concern? Ask yourself, "What is this like? What does this remind me of?"

When it comes to interpreting the symbolic language of your daydream, you are your own best expert. If you believe you had a genuine response experience but the meaning was not clear, was confusing, or seemed unrelated to your request, what is your best guess as to its meaning? Imagine you know. You can always explore further using the advanced contemplation techniques you learned.

Finally, as Thurston (1978) reminded, the real dream interpretation comes when you begin to apply the daydream in your daily life. Consider or contemplate what (if anything) will change in your life as a result of applying this new information and/or insight? In your imagination, implement the response received. How does that feel? How could you turn this insight into action? List several ways you might practically act on the response to create a better life (Johnson, 1986). Make a plan for carrying out your choice. Mentally rehearse your plan using the technique of contemplation learned. Consider the advice given, but do not delegate your responsibility. Evaluate the risks and benefits before taking physical action. You are responsible for the choices you make. If it feels right, then put the advice into physical action.

> *"The art of communication lies in listening."* –
> Malcom Forbes

Conclusion

You have now been introduced to all 7 steps in the transformational daydreaming system. At this point, in relation to your understanding and skills, do you feel consciously incompetent or consciously competent? Most people would probably state their level of competence lay somewhere between these two choices. With review, repetition, and lots of practice, you may be pleasantly surprised to discover just how quickly your competence will improve.

Stick to the system as it is presented. Use it. It's like a path that's been hacked out of the jungle for you. Stay on the trail because it leads right to the destination you want. The goal is communication with the subconscious mind.

Remember you cannot fail. You can only learn. You're honing a skill that you'll be able to use for the rest of your life to improve all of your life. And if it takes you a few weeks or even a few months, great! That's a brilliant use of your time and a wonderful investment in your future.

If you respect the ritual of the overall process, you'll eventually discover it takes on a life of its own, strengthens your intent, and makes it easier for you to successfully communicate. Try it. Test it. Prove it. Your subconscious is willing to communicate with you but are you listening?

Once you've had the opportunity to study, learn, and practice the entire process another 6-12 times or more, you'll be ready to explore and experiment with some of the more than 37 different applications described in chapter 10.

If you have not already done so, I suggest you photocopy the *Master List of Main Points for Preview and Review* located at the back of this book. Place the pages together in a binder for ease of reference.

And now, the moment you've been waiting for. For the first time, in the next chapter, instructions for completing all 7-steps of the transformational daydreaming process will be presented.

Again, congrats for your good work! Keep going. Why settle for mediocrity when mastery lay straight ahead?

Main Points for Preview and Review

- ✓ In this chapter, you learned the 4 remaining steps of the 7-step transformational daydreaming process. These steps are: (4) Receive a Daydream; (5) Reorient; (6) Exit Your Safe Place; and (7) Document, Analyze, and Interpret Your Experience.

- ✓ After you study, learn, and practice all 7 steps, you'll be able to explore and experiment with more than 37 different applications for communicating with your super-intelligence within. These and other suggestions are explored in chapter 10.

- ✓ You learned to begin to recognize the shift that takes place when transitioning from contemplation to spontaneous daydreaming.

- ✓ Your progress using the transformational daydreaming process is rarely linear. It's more realistic to expect a zig-zag journey full of unexpected twists and turns. Knowing this ahead of time will help you avoid disappointment or worse still, blaming yourself for "not doing it right." Learn from your experience. Keep trying. There is no failure, only feedback.

- ✓ Initially you may experience virtually no spontaneous daydreams. That's okay, because with practice, you'll most likely begin experiencing the glimpses and hints described. It's possible that one day you may even experience the holy grail of daydream experiences—the full, spontaneous, and lucid daydream.

- ✓ To improve your daydream recall, the most helpful task you can do is to write it down as soon as you finish your session. The physical act of writing it down helps cement it into your memory and demonstrates that you value the information shared.

- ✓ When reflecting and interpreting your daydreams, you will often experience an "aha." You want to pay special attention to the "aha" moments that are new, novel, and surprising—something that takes you beyond what you already knew.

- ✓ When it comes to interpreting the symbolic language of your daydream, you are your own best expert.

- ✓ The real daydream interpretation comes when you begin to apply the daydream in your daily life. Consider or contemplate what (if anything) will change in your life as a result of applying this new information and/or insight. How could you turn this insight into action?

- ✓ Carefully consider any information you receive from your subconscious mind. Respect the advice given but do not delegate responsibility. You are responsible for the decisions and choices you make, and for the actions you take.

- ✓ In chapter 9, complete instructions for using all 7-steps of the transformational daydreaming process is presented.

References

Barth, D. (1997). *Unlock the creative power of daydreams.* NY, NY: Penguin Group.

Delaney, G. (1996). *Living your dreams.* NY, NY: HarperCollins.

Feinstein, D., & Krippner, S. (2006). *The mythic path.* Santa Rosa, CA: Energy Psychology Press.

Johnson, R. (1986). *Inner work using dreams and active imagination for personal growth.* NY, NY: Harper One.

Taylor, J. (2009). *The wisdom of your dreams.* NY, NY: The Penguin Group.

Thurston, M. (1978). *How to interpret your dreams.* Virginia Beach, VA: A.R.E. Press.

Timothy A. Storlie, PhD

CHAPTER 9

THE COMPLETE 7-STEP PROCESS OF TRANSFORMATIONAL DAYDREAMING

Welcome to chapter 9. You stand and face the future with a desire for more information and insight about a specific concern.

You've studied, practiced, and waited patiently to arrive at this point. All your theoretical preparation and practical work is now complete. Here, for the first time, is the entire 7-step process for communicating with your subconscious mind and receiving insights into how you can create a better life.

Your Mini-Manual

Think of this chapter as your mini-manual. It's what you reach for when learning and practicing the 7-steps—when you want to communicate with your subconscious mind. For your convenience, this mini-manual is also included in the *Master List of Chapter Points for Review* located at the end of this book. This makes it easy for you to photocopy and use these instructions to help you explore, experiment, and experience the 7-step transformational daydreaming process.

As you read through this chapter for the first time, the idea that you could memorize all these instructions may seem like a daunting task. Believe me, after you have read and followed these guidelines 20-30 times, you'll likely have them memorized. This is a goal worth working toward because as your memorization of instructions will free you to be more mindful of your internal experience.

Ready? Here we go ...

Step 1 – Go to your Safe Place

It begins with hope. Similar to the picture of the boy displayed on the first page of this chapter, you stand and face the future with a desire for more information, insight, and inspiration about a specific concern.

Full of this hope, desire, and expectancy, sit or lie down, close your eyes, and imagine entering your Safe Place. Using the method you learned in chapter 5, mentally repeat the name of your Safe Place 3 times. With all your senses , imagine being there now. Make your experience as real as possible. Mentally repeat the phrase, *"safe, relaxed, comfortable."* Feel comfortable and confident as your brain automatically begins to produce more alpha brainwaves. After approximately 60-90 seconds, continue with the next step.

Step 2 – Relax and Enter an Altered State

Use the *countdown-to-relaxation method*. For your ease of reference, it's repeated here. Eventually, it would be preferable if you could complete all steps from memory. But don't worry. There's no hurry.

To memorize these guidelines, most people will need to read through these instructions many times and carry out much mindful practice spread out over a dozen or more sessions. Use the accelerated learning techniques from chapter 3 to help speed up the development of your competency.

 a. Continue to sit or lie comfortably with your eyes gently closed. Focus your relaxed awareness around your heart area and think, *"As I mentally count down from 7 to 1, I relax more deeply and enter an altered state."* Begin the countdown. Notice (or simply imagine) that with each number you count, you begin to feel more safe, relaxed, and calm. Complete one easy breath for each number you count. As you inhale, think the specific number (or imagine seeing it written on a black or white-board). As you exhale, think the word, *"calm."* Practice this step now.

 b. With your eyes still closed, keep breathing and mentally counting down. After you reach the number 1, pause to recall any relaxing personal memory for about 20-30 seconds (for example, a relaxing memory from a recent vacation, relaxing in mediation, sitting next to a lake). Practice this step now.

c. With your eyes still closed, begin to deepen your altered state of awareness by mentally repeating three times, *"I feel safe, relaxed and comfortable ... I feel safe, relaxed, and comfortable ... I feel safe, relaxed, and comfortable."* Practice this step now.

d. To further deepen your altered state, place your hands on your lap and touch the tip of each index finger gently to the tip of each thumb.

With your eyes still closed, mentally suggest, *"As I count down from 3 to 1, I go deeper into an altered state of awareness. And when I reach the number 1, I'll be in a deeply altered state of awareness."* Without physically moving your head, gently shift your eyes to your right and imagine seeing the number 3 there. With your attention on the right side, slowly and mentally count *"3 ... 3 ... 3."* With your head remaining still, shift your eyes and look to the middle of your visual field—straight out in front of you. With your attention relaxed yet fixed in the middle of your visual field, see the number 2 there. Slowly and mentally count *"2

... 2 ... 2." With your head physically still, shift your eyes gently to the left side of your visual field, see the number 1, and slowly, mentally count "1 ... 1 ... 1." Now rest in a deeply altered state. After 1-2 minutes, continue with step 3. Practice this step now.

Step 3 – Contemplate to Communicate with Subconscious Mind

This is when you ask the subconscious to listen to your concerns. In order for the subconscious mind to respond with a daydream, you first have to connect with it. Using its name—and with your eyes still closed—mentally call out to your subconscious mind. Imagine your subconscious mind—this super power of information and intelligence—is listening. Greet your subconscious mind respectfully and state your purpose. For example, "Hello (name). Thank you for all you do. I would like your help with (your concern). Begin by mentally explaining what you want and why—2 or 3 sentences is plenty. For example, *"I want to write a book about communicating with my subconscious mind using contemplation and daydreaming. I believe many people will benefit from having access to this information."* That's it. Don't overthink it. After your mental request and explanation, begin to contemplate (communicate) using the multi-sensory imagery process you learned previously in chapter 7. This is how you "talk" to the subconscious mind. This is how you communicate the details of your concern or question. You do it with your contemplation.

A detailed contemplation provides your subconscious with a multi-sensory impression of your concern. Your contemplation conveys your request and shows the subconscious what you desire.

Contemplate over your request for a few minutes (or for as long as feels right). Combine process imagery to illustrate how your desire might potentially come into being with end-state imagery to showcase the desired outcome—how it looks when it's done or complete. Feel it. Make it as real as possible. Depending on the nature of your request to the subconscious mind, your contemplation could depict a possible beginning, middle, and an end of your desire or concern.

You are contemplating. You hope your subconscious mind will respond with a daydream. This daydream response may come when you've finished your contemplation, not at all, or during your contemplation. You need to be open to timing of your subconscious mind's response.

When the subconscious mind begins to respond, there are many ways you might experience the subtle shift from your directed contemplation to the spontaneous daydream of the subconscious mind. Remember, the subconscious mind could begin to respond while you are still contemplating. If it begins to take over your contemplation and shift to a daydream while you are still contemplating, you need to recognize this is occurring. Carefully read the example below to gain more clarity of how this shift might feel. This can help you learn to recognize when this shift begins so you won't miss it.

Here is one example of how it may feel when this shift from active contemplation to spontaneous daydreaming occurs.

You're sitting with eyes closed in your Safe Place. You feel relaxed and in an altered state. You've asked the subconscious mind for help, and now you're consciously contemplating on your desire. During contemplation, there are moments when your mind seems to wander. You become aware you're not contemplating in the same way you were a moment ago—you're thinking about something completely different. It's as if you catch yourself contemplating upon a different topic. You catch a glimpse of images or maybe the hint of a sound that you didn't purposely choose, and you didn't consciously imagine. These glimpses may or may not be a response from your subconscious mind but pat close attention anyway so that you can recall and document them in the final step 7. Your analysis and interpretation will help you discern if these experiences were a response to your concerns.

As you become more relaxed and drift into a deeper altered state, these momentary lapses often increase. They could even develop into a completely spontaneous daydream. This is a good sign — almost certainly a response from your subconscious mind. Back off your contemplation and allow the subconscious mind full and free reign. If this occurs, your detached observation is a must. Why? Because some people get excited at this point, and guess what? The curtain closes. They lose awareness of the daydream. Why? Too much conscious mind present. This is exactly the point where detached curiosity is critical. Feelings of excitement can shift control away from the subconscious mind back to the conscious mind — just the opposite of what you're trying to do.

Your goal is to receive a response from your subconscious mind in the form of a daydream. Whether your subconscious mind responds *during* your contemplation or *after* you have finished your contemplation, to succeed in this approach, it is critical that you follow the guidelines explained in step 4 below.

Step 4 – Receive a Daydream from Your Subconscious Mind

Stop contemplating. Patiently, passively, and receptively sit, wait, and pay attention. Watch. Listen. Wait for the subconscious to respond. Sit with a curious attitude of detached expectancy and remain open to what might happen, no matter how mundane or surprising.

Allow the subconscious mind complete freedom and autonomy to direct the daydreaming process with no conscious interference from you. This communication process has virtually no chance of succeeding unless you're willing to take your hands off the steering wheel, allow the subconscious mind to show up when it's good and ready, take its place in the driver's seat, and drive the bus free of your judgment and micro-management. [FYI - this is easier said than done.]

Allow any daydreaming activity to unfold spontaneously. Be receptive to what occurs. Remember, the response from your subconscious mind can range from nothing at all: to a glimpse of faint and confusing images; a mixed grab bag of personal memories; barely audible words or sounds; subtle impressions, sensations, or feelings; and any and all possible combinations of these experiences; all the way to the experience of a full mental movie. When step 4 feels complete, you've had enough, or nothing has occurred within a reasonable amount of time, you can begin to close the daydreaming process.

Many people require several attempts before noticing any subconscious response. If no recognizable response is forthcoming within 10-20 minutes,

- Thank the subconscious mind for listening.
- Ask the subconscious mind for its help in recognizing its response when it does come.

- Follow the steps to conclude your session.
- Try another day and trust that every step you take, takes you a step closer to success.

Step 5 – Return to Normal, Wakeful Awareness

When the daydream feels complete or you have decided to conclude your session for other reasons, what do you do? You thank your subconscious mind and begin the process of returning to your ordinary state of normal, wakeful awareness. Mentally suggest to yourself that in the next few seconds, when you open your eyes, you will feel awake, alert, fully conscious, and with excellent recall of whatever you may have experienced..

Step 6 – Exit Your Safe Place

Before leaving, remind yourself that you can return to your Safe Place anytime you want by simply intending to, closing your eyes, and mentally repeating the name of your Safe Place three times. Then, gently open your eyes, bringing all of your experiences, learnings, insights, and "aha's" with you.

Step 7 – Document, Analyze, and Interpret Your Daydream

Please stop! Do not engage in any other activity until you complete this final step. Why? Because daydreams are like night dreams. Both are easily forgotten and can quickly evaporate in the presence of competing thoughts. After all…

What's the point of completing this 7-step process for communicating with your subconscious mind if afterword you can't recall the advice given?

To improve your daydream recall, the most helpful task you can do is to write your daydream down immediately after you finish your session.

The physical act of writing it down helps cement it into your memory.

Write down only what you can specifically recall of your daydream experience. This is not the time for guesswork, speculation, or interpretation. That will come later. Like the dreams of the night, the dreams of the day are symbolic (Barth, 1997). Yet daydream interpretation involves much more than simply translating symbols.

Remember a daydream can range from a glimpse of vague images, feelings, sensations, sounds, smells, and fleeting personal memories, to a full mental movie. What did you experience specifically? As you record your daydream, regard everything you experienced as potentially useful information. Assume all aspects of your daydream were symbolically related to your concern. Write everything you can recall down on paper before proceeding. Just the facts as you recall them. Simply describe your actual experience.

When you have recorded as much as you can honestly recall, then ask yourself if you believe your subconscious responded to your request for help. Did it respond? If your answer is yes, take a moment to celebrate that it really happened. This is an important achievement you can build and expand upon.

If you believe you had a genuine response from the subconscious mind, then the next most important task is to begin the process of daydream interpretation. Ask, "What is this daydream trying to tell me?" (Feinstein & Krippner, 2006).

Reflect on your daydream in its entirety. Try to capture the holistic essence of its message by summarizing what you can recall into a single phrase or sentence—similar to the title of a movie.

Again, ask, "what is this daydream trying to tell me?" What comes to you when you ask this question? How does the daydream make you feel? What does it remind you of?

Did this daydream provide you with any immediate, obvious, fresh insight into your concern? If so, describe this insight with as much detail as you feel is helpful. What was your subconscious trying to tell you? What is the single most important insight this response is trying to communicate to you? You are building toward an interpretation and there could be more than one.

A note of caution, especially if you received a lot of information. When working toward daydream interpretation, favor insights and information that are creative, new, novel, and surprising. Also, when reflecting upon your daydream—in its entirety or in its parts—you will often experience an "aha."

Taylor, (2009) describes the "aha" recognition as a trustworthy guide to discovering authentic, accurate interpretations but cautions that the initial aha moments are likely to occur over things you already know or recognize. The treasure lies in the sense of surprise—the "aha" that takes you beyond what you already know. Delaney (1996) agrees. She writes, "You will know that you have succeeded in interpreting your dream when it tells you something you did not realize before." After all, why would your subconscious mind waste time communicating something you already think you know? Be cautious of responses that only seem to confirm what you already know, believe, or suspect.

Next, look at the individual parts and symbols of the daydream. List the people, places, activities, images, sounds, sensations, emotions, you observed. What feelings do you have about each of these images? What words or ideas come to mind when you recall this image? Do you feel energized by this image? Does this image remind you of anything that is connected to your concern? Ask yourself, "What is this like? What does this remind me of?"

When it comes to interpreting the symbolic language of your daydream, you are your own best expert. If you believe you had a genuine response experience but the meaning was confusing or seemed unrelated to your request, what is your best guess as to its meaning? Pretend you know. You can always contemplate further upon this using the advanced techniques you learned.

Finally, as Thurston (1978) reminded, the real dream interpretation comes when you begin to discover applications of daydream insights in your daily life. How could you turn insight into action? Consider or contemplate what (if anything) will change in your life as a result of applying this new information and/or insight. In your imagination, implement the response received. How does that feel?

List several ways you might practically act on the response to create a better life (Johnson, 1986). Make a plan for carrying out your choice. Mentally rehearse your plan using the technique of contemplation learned. Consider the advice given, but do not delegate your responsibility. Evaluate the risk and benefits before taking physical action. You are responsible for the decisions you make and the actions you take.

This final step of *Document, Analyze, and Interpret Your Daydream* may seem long, confusing, and cumbersome to you. If so, please don't worry. There's a simple explanation and solution. The explanation can be found in the 4-stage model for developing competency explained in chapter 3.

According to the 4-stage model, since you've just been exposed to a lot of new information, any feelings of confusion you may have are normal. Why? Because at this stage of your learning about how to conduct daydream analysis and interpretation, you are probably operating at the level of *conscious incompetence*. Yes, you are acquiring theoretical knowledge about daydream interpretation, but you have yet to actually do it.

You simply lack the required experience at this point. That is the explanation. The solution follows next.

The solution to any confusion is deep, deliberate practice. If you use the principles of deep practice (as discussed in chapter 3), to further develop your skills of daydream analysis and interpretation, the 4-stage model for developing competency, predicts you will evolve from the second stage of *conscious incompetence* to the third stage of learning—*conscious competence*. And after that, even further. The key is your deep, deliberate practice.

And remember, when faced with a problem or concern, you can always ask the magic question, *"How can I use transformational daydreaming to help me improve my skills of daydream analysis and interpretation?"*

If you understand, respect, and apply the structure and ritual of the overall 7-step process, you'll eventually discover it takes on a life of its own, strengthens your intent, and makes it easier for you to successfully communicate with your subconscious mind. Try it. Test it. Prove it. Your subconscious is willing to communicate with you but are you listening?

Once again, congratulations! You've not only learned the entire 7-step transformational daydreaming process, you've assembled an impressive set of tools that you can begin to use to help create a better personal and/or professional life. This collection of tools and techniques is the main focus of the next chapter.

Main Points for Preview and Review

- ✓ Your theoretical preparation and practical work is now complete. Here, for the first time, is the entire 7-step process for communicating with your subconscious mind and receiving insights into how you can create a better life.

- ✓ Think of this chapter as a mini-manual for communicating with your subconscious mind. For your convenience, this entire mini-manual is also included in the *Master List of Chapter Points for Preview and Review* located at the end of this book. This will make it easy for you to photocopy and use these instructions.

- ✓ If you understand, respect, and apply the structure and ritual of the overall 7-step process, you'll eventually discover it takes on a life of its own, strengthens your intent, and makes it easier for you to successfully communicate with your subconscious mind. Try it. Test it. Prove it. Your subconscious is willing to communicate with you but are you listening?

- ✓ Once again, congratulations! You've not only learned the entire 7-step transformational daydreaming process, you've assembled an impressive set of tools that you can begin to use to help create a better personal and/or professional life. This collection of tools and techniques is the main focus of the next chapter.

References

Barth, D. (1997). *Unlock the creative power of daydreams.* NY, NY: Penguin Group.

Bosnak, R. (1988). *A little course in dreams.* Boston, MS: Shambhala.

Delaney, G. (1996). *Living your dreams.* NY, NY: HarperCollins.

Feinstein, D., & Krippner, S. (2006). *The mythic path.* Santa Rosa, CA: Energy Psychology Press.

Johnson, R. (1986). *Inner work using dreams and active imagination for personal growth.* NY, NY: Harper One.

Taylor, J. (2009). *The wisdom of your dreams.* NY, NY: The Penguin Group.

Thurston, M. (1978). *How to interpret your dreams.* Virginia Beach, VA: A.R.E. Press.

Timothy A. Storlie, PhD

CHAPTER 10

37 APPLICATIONS AND 22 TOOLS

This chapter lists 22 tools and more than 37 ways you can apply your new skills and tools. You will probably come up with even more. All you need to do is keep an open mind, explore, experiment, ask a lot of questions, and …

Think Outside the Box!

The Questions You Ask, Determine the Answers You Get

What are some novel ways you could use the various tools and techniques you have learned? Are certain tools and techniques better suited for some tasks over others? How could you combine various techniques to help you create the better life you desire? Do you have a specific concern right now? If so, which of the 22 tools might be of help to you?

The following section and exercise is designed to help you consider how you might answer the above questions. Again, the answers you get depend on the questions you ask.

Want a higher quality answer?
Ask a higher quality question.

Inventory Your Tools, Techniques, and Skills

Many useful tools have been shared—tools you can use to improve nearly any area of your life. The purpose of the following exercise is to help stimulate your creative thinking and expand your awareness of how the tools you have learned might be helpful.

Exercise

A. Read through the list of the 22 tools, techniques, and methods that are presented.
B. After reviewing the list of tools, read the section, *The Answers You get Depend on the Questions You Ask*.
C. Next, insert each of the 22 tools (one by one) into each of the questions posed.
D. Reflect on many ways each tool can be used to help create a better personal and/or professional life. For example, the first question is "How can you use the skills you have learned to improve your physical health, strength,

flexibility, and stamina?" Look at the first tool listed (*Accelerated learning*) and contemplate over "How could you use accelerated learning to improve your physical health, strength, flexibility, and stamina?" Some tools will be a better fit with some questions.

List of Tools

1. Accelerated learning.
2. Your Safe Place.
3. Multi-sensory mental imagery.
4. Countdown to relaxation.
5. Countdown into an altered state of awareness.
6. Self-suggestion.
7. Contemplation.
8. Daydreaming.
9. Preview, review, read, and repeat.
10. Power of questions.
11. Intuition.
12. Igniting motivation.
13. 4 stages of developing competence.
14. Deep, deliberate practice.
15. Strengthening neural connections.
16. Mudra.
17. Active imagery, receptive imagery, process imagery, and end-state imagery.
18. Self-talk.
19. Applications of forward and backward chaining.
20. Imaginal conversations.
21. The lunar cycle.
22. Transformational daydreaming communication process.

List of Sample Questions to Ask with Each Tool

A. How you can use _____ to improve your physical health, wellness, strength, flexibility, and stamina?
B. What are some ways you could use _____ to improve your diet, exercise and sleep?
C. How could use _____ to help improve your piano, guitar, or drum playing?
D. What are some ways you could use _____ to improve your favorite sports or recreational activity?
E. How could use _____ to help reduce fear, worry, depression, and/or anxiety?
F. What are some ways you could use _____ to improve memory, focus, concentration, creativity, and imagination?
G. What are some ways you could use _____ to conduct paranormal, transpersonal, and spiritual experiments?
H. How could you use _____ to envision new business products and services?
I. What are some of the ways you could use _____ to improve communications and relations?
J. How could you use _____ to become a better listener?
K. How could you can use _____ to cultivate patience?
L. What are some of the ways you could use _____ to feel more centered and balanced?
M. How could _____ be used to increase feelings of hopefulness and optimism?
N. What are some of the ways you could use _____ to improve critical thinking and reasoning?
O. What are some ways you could use _____ to cultivate spiritual qualities, such as loving-kindness, compassion, gratitude, altruism, and ability to forgive?

P. How might _____ be used to deepen prayer, contemplation, meditation, expand awareness and a felt-sense of connection and oneness?

Q. What are some ways you could use _____ to help achieve self-realization and enlightenment?

R. How could you use _____ to experience and develop mystical, paranormal, psychic, and transpersonal abilities?

S. How could you use _____ to address any of the 37 issues listed in the section *Sample of Areas You Can Explore, Experiment, and Experience?*

Again, the answers you get, depend
on the questions you ask

---

37 Areas You Can Explore, Experiment, and Experience

Improve Physical Well-Being and Enhance Performance

- Improve physical health and wellness.
- Improve strength, stamina, flexibility, and speed.
- Improve your diet, exercise and sleep.
- Enhance practice of any sports or recreational activity.
- Enhance your practice of any hobby, e.g., photography.
- Enhance musical or artistic performance.

Improve Emotional Health and Relationships

- Improve emotional health and well-being.
- Increase trust, openness and intimacy.
- Develop greater communication fluency and competency.
- Reduce anxiety, panic, and worry.
- Help reduce or overcome phobias and fears.
- Reduce feelings of depression.
- Feel more relaxed, calm and centered.
- Increase personal motivation.
- Feel more optimistic and hopeful.
- Improve feelings about your physical appearance.
- Increase your self-confidence and self-esteem.
- Enhance romance, eroticism, and sexual intimacy.

Improve Mental Abilities and Enhance Creativity

- Increase memory, focus, concentration.
- Stretch your imagination.

- Ignite personal and professional creativity in numerous areas. For example, writers can use contemplation to discover solutions to outline, plot, or character development. You can use it to explore alternative story or movie endings.
- Relive, review, or alter memories. For example, you can use contemplation and daydreaming to vividly review and reminisce memories and experiences—old boyfriends or girlfriends, accomplishments from your past, things that you're proud of, your achievements. Dwell on what makes you feel good. Reminisce in vivid detail about the signature moments of your life—all your "firsts." When you got married, when you had your first kid, when you graduated from this school or that program, when you built your first house, or when you did anything that you were proud of, that made you feel good and competent. It's good to think about these things from time to time. To reminisce over your highlights—your signature moments—promotes health and wellness.
- Accelerate learning.
- Conduct numerous paranormal, transpersonal, and spiritual experiments (described in detail in chapter 11).

Business and Professional Development

- Professional development.
- Envision and create a new business, service, or product.
- Improve professional service delivery.
- Enhance and support corporate culture.
- Develop professional plans, goals, and objectives.
- Increase customer, client, or patient satisfaction.
- Improve management, marketing, and sales.
- Improve recruiting, interviewing, hiring, and staff training.
- Use imaginal interactions to improve negotiations, rehearse future conversations, meetings, and presentations.

- Team building, employee motivation and retention.
- Improve specific work-related skills.
- Explore and experiment with novel approaches.
- Try out new career or job possibilities.

Imaginal Conversations

Many of the options above make use of imaginal conversations. Imaginal conversations allow you the freedom to experiment with various communication approaches. This can be helpful when you feel nervous or upset. It can also be helpful when discussing sensitive or confrontational topics—in your personal, intimate relationships and with business colleagues.

People often use mental rehearsal to prepare for future, personal or professional conversations and meetings. I've done this many times when I had to give a presentation, or appear before a committee, a board, and/or explain a proposal. It really helps, if nothing else, to calm your nerves.

Because you want to deliver your message as clearly and competently as possible, it often helps to mentally rehearse these conversations. How? Go to your Safe Place, relax, enter an altered state and use multi-sensory contemplation to imagine yourself interacting with this person. During imaginal conversation, it is important to:

- Be in the picture. Look out through your eyes as if there.
- Have a conversation.
- Hear yourself talking.
- Hear the other person responding.
- Notice the looks on the other person's face.
- Explore different approaches and see how each feels.
- Adjust what you say, how you say it and notice how that affects the conversation.
- Adjust your approach until you get the response you hope for. If one approach does not produce the outcome you desire, rewind and try another.

Viagra for the Mind

You can enhance romance, eroticism, and intimate pleasure at any adult age. There's kind of a joke that sexual fantasies function similar to a Viagra for the mind. That's pretty accurate! Imagery can have a dramatic effect on the body. You probably already know that.

Conclusion

Contemplation, intentional daydreaming, communicating with the subconscious mind—these are all skills you can use for the rest of your life to improve the quality of nearly every aspect of your life. If there's anything you are curious about, interested in, or want to learn or improve, why not also explore the topic using your contemplation skills?

If you're looking for answers, insight, more information, possible applications, why not take the next step and "discuss" it with your subconscious mind—the super-intelligence within you? Who knows? Maybe the subconscious will provide you with some information that's helpful.

List of Main Points for Preview and Review

- ✓ You now have an impressive set of tools you can use to help improve nearly every aspect of your life—personal, professional, physical, emotional, mental, social, sexual, financial, creative, philosophical, metaphysical, mystical, psychic, transpersonal, and spiritual.

- ✓ This chapter lists 22 tools and techniques that were presented (see the *Master List of Chapter Main Points* located at the end of this book).

- ✓ 37 areas that you can explore, experiment, and experience are listed under the categories of physical, emotional and relationships, intellectual and mental, business and professional, and imaginal conversations.

- ✓ The questions you ask, determine the answers you get. Want a higher quality answer? Ask a higher quality question?

- ✓ For the rest of your life, you can use your skills to improve the quality of nearly every aspect of your life.

CHAPTER 11

PSYCHIC, SPIRITUAL, AND TRANSPERSONAL DAYDREAMING—THE SKY'S THE LIMIT

The alpha brainwaves associated with daydreaming may also be related to hypnosis, paranormal, psychic phenomena, spiritual, and transpersonal experiences.

Mysterious Brainwaves

When you are contemplating and/or daydreaming in a relaxed, altered state of awareness, your brain increases production of alpha brainwaves. In addition to daydreaming, alpha brainwaves are also associated with hypnotic states, and various mystical, paranormal, psychic, spiritual, and transpersonal phenomena (Krippner, Bogzaran & De Carvalho, 2002).

Paranormal experiences refer to events currently beyond traditional scientific explanation. *Psychic* perception means mysterious, extraordinary understanding, perception, and/or sensitivity to non-physical, supernatural forces and influences. *Spiritual* refers to sacred matters and/or religious values. *Transpersonal* focuses on those experiences that transcend the usual sense of self or personal identity (Mish, 2009).

This chapter introduces you to some of the many ways you could use the transformational daydreaming process to explore the realms of the paranormal, enhance your psychic perception, cultivate spiritual values, and experience the transpersonal. You'll never know what you can do with your imagination until you try.

One final time, as you study this chapter, be sure to read with the *new* key question in mind.

"How can I use transformational daydreaming to help me _____ ?"

There's Always One More ...

Here's one example that illustrates how contemplation can unexpectedly lead to the experience of insight and expansion of awareness. One summer afternoon, a long time ago, I was lying on the couch. It was the middle of the afternoon and I was feeling lazy. Thinking about something I read, I closed my eyes and started contemplating on the concept of reincarnation. Head nodding and nearly asleep, my subconscious mind began generating spontaneous daydreams ...

Transformational Daydreaming

Walking barefoot along a white, sandy beach, I spotted what I guessed were ancient ruins. The scene changed. I was climbing a ladder extending up through the clouds into the blue sky. A mist appeared from nowhere. Standing still on a ladder's rung, all I could see was the next step immediately above and below me.

I heard a male voice say, *"on the infinite ladder of perfection, there's always one more."* An outstretched hand appeared from the swirling mist. Grabbing it, I held firm.

Seconds later, another hand appeared—this one reaching up from the veiled rung below. I extended a helping hand. Whoever it was, grabbed me and held on tight. At that moment, I felt the truth of the ancient Druid's prayer—that within infinite space, where everything is connected and one—we stand heart to heart, hand in hand, united in spirit, together we stand.

Then an aha insight occurred that would last a lifetime. I realized that on the climb up the ladder of life, there is no final rung. There's *always* one more step to take. And as we climb, we mutually benefit from each other's willingness to give and receive.

Spiritual and Transpersonal Contemplation and Daydreaming

Just as I had unexpectedly benefited from the above contemplation to achieve greater insight, understanding, and awareness, so do countless artists, metaphysicians, mystics, writers and others also use and benefit from contemplation and daydreaming as part of their creative process. And if you want, you can too.

It begins with hope. It continues by developing the view that such things are possible as explained in chapter two. As always, your interpretation matters. How you view something makes a difference.

The Magic Question

If you're interested in metaphysical, paranormal, psychic, spiritual, and/or transpersonal matters, you can use the transformational daydreaming process to help imagine, explore, learn, enhance, experiment, and possibly experience. Just ask the magic questions:

- How could I use transformational daydreaming to deepen meditation and altered states of awareness?
- How could I use transformational daydreaming to increase expression of virtuous qualities such as altruism, compassion, forgiveness, hope, gratitude, kindness, love, mindfulness, patience, and wisdom?
- How could I use transformational daydreaming to enhance experience and appreciation of balance, beauty, and harmony?
- How could I use transformational daydreaming to help expand consciousness and increase illumination, self-realization, and enlightenment?
- How could I use transformational daydreaming to improve my psychic and transpersonal skills such as

beyond-the-body travel, distance healing, divination, intuition, remote viewing, time-travel, and/or telepathy?
- How could I use transformational daydreaming to increase my insight into religious, spiritual, metaphysical, and cosmic mysteries, questions, and concerns such as prayer, karma, reincarnation, life after death, connection, oneness, and unity?
- How could I use transformational daydreaming to ....

In your inner world of daydreams, you can experience bold, new adventures without risk.

Within the realms of imagination, past, present, and future are all arenas for possible exploration. You might visit with ancestors, deceased friends, and/or famous personalities. You could explore the possibilities of past lives. You could attempt to meet and talk with your "future self." You could experiment with magically attracting what you desire, repelling what you don't. You could conduct thought experiments as Albert Einstein was fond of doing. All these options and others, may be available to you if you desire, hope, intend, study, learn, practice, explore, and experiment over time.

All this and more might be possible because you learned to befriend and communicate with the subconscious mind — the super intelligence within you.

Exercise: Develop Your Intuition

Imagine you want to enhance your intuition. You decide to use the tools and techniques from transformational daydreaming to help you accomplish this. Here's one possible approach (slightly different than the 7-steps you previously learned, yet very similar).

1. You begin with your hope and desire for increased knowledge, insight, inspiration, and experience of intuition.

2. Close your eyes and imagine going to your Safe Place. Repeat its name three times. Feel safe, comfortable, and relaxed as your brainwaves begin to shift toward alpha.

3. Relax and enter an altered state of awareness. Do this by means of the *Countdown to Relaxation* and the *Deepen Your Altered State* method.

4. Gently begin to communicate your desire for enhanced intuition to the subconscious mind using multi-sensory contemplation. Call to your subconscious mind by using its name. Think about intuition—the final outcome you desire. Ponder on it. Mull it over. What would enhanced intuition feel like to you? What does this mean to you? Imagine some of the ways you would use enhanced intuition to improve your personal and professional life, such as improving communication with your spouse, resolving a current health concern, or improving your investment portfolio. This is how you ask for help. When the subconscious mind is ready to respond to your request, it uses spontaneous daydreaming.

5. Patiently, passively, and receptively sit, wait, and pay attention. Wait for the subconscious to respond. Watch. Listen. Be receptive to what occurs—anything from a glimpse of a faint image to the experience of a richly-detailed mental movie. Responses may come as thoughts, memories, images, sounds, feelings, sensations, dreams, daydreams, and/or any combination of the above.

6. When your contemplation feels complete, follow the steps you learned previously on how to come out of an altered

state and awaken yourself. Exit your Safe Place bringing all your learning, insights, and "aha's" with you. Consciously come back to where you are physically, fully alert, and fully awake.

7. Open your eyes. Write a brief summary of your experience. Document, analyze, and interpret your results as you learned. Do what is required to turn insight into action.

In the coming days, continue to think and learn about intuition. Practice. Wishing is not enough! Use supportive self-talk, multi-sensory mental rehearsal. Remember the importance of *doing* in developing competence and mastery. You might even consider a creative approach to "befriending" intuition — something similar to the process you used when you befriended the subconscious mind.

The exercise above provides an example of a general process you could use to begin to experience, explore, and experiment with any topic of interest and importance to you. You are free to explore! Just ask the magic question … "How I could use transformational daydreaming to _____?"

Consider the Lunar Cycle

When it comes to transpersonal and psychic experiences and skill development, some people believe that it is important to consider the lunar cycle. For example, if you want to attract or increase a skill, supposedly, the ideal time to use contemplation and transformational daydreaming is during the moon's two-week waxing time. This is the time from the New Moon to the Full Moon.

And the best time to use contemplation and daydreaming to repel or get rid of things that you don't want in your life, is during the two-week waning time. This is the time from the Full Moon to the New Moon.

It's very easy to track the lunar cycle. You can find free apps for your PC, tablet, or Smart Phone that will display what phase of the lunar cycle you are in for your exact location. Why not experiment to see what difference (if any) it makes?

A Frequently Asked Question and Answer

Q: If I use the transformational daydreaming process to help develop a psychic skill, say for example, intuition, how can I integrate the Lunar cycle into my sessions?

A: First, focus on learning the system as presented. Then, on the exact day of the New Moon (the first day of the waxing lunar cycle—the 14-day period from the New Moon to Full Moon)—finish one session focused on your desire (in this example, intuition).

Then, keeping your same desire (intuition), complete another session every 2-3 days throughout the remainder of the 2-week waxing cycle. This means you would complete a total of 5-7 sessions during this 2 week phase of the lunar cycle.

After completing this series of sessions, wait until the next New Moon and then repeat the entire process all over again. In other words, focus on your intention (intuition) over 2-3 complete lunar cycles.

During this time, use your intuition. Pretend and act as if it's already well developed. Pay attention. See what happens. Write down your results.

Summing Up

In this chapter, you learned that the alpha brainwaves associated with daydreaming are also related to hypnotic states, transpersonal experiences, and psychic phenomena such as intuition, remote viewing, and telepathy.

You discovered you can use contemplation and daydreaming to explore and experiment with developing and deepening numerous psychic, mystical paranormal, spiritual, transpersonal skills and abilities. And you learned how to experiment timing your contemplation and paranormal daydreaming sessions with the lunar cycle.

This book began with the hope that you could (and would) create a better life. Along the way, you discovered that transformational daydreaming is a special way of using the power of your imagination. Most importantly, you learned to cultivate a special friendship with your subconscious mind—the super intelligence that dwells within you. You learned that when you want to communicate with the subconscious mind, you use contemplation, and that when the subconscious mind wants to communicate with you, it uses spontaneous daydreams.

"A daily dose of daydreaming heals the heart, soothes the soul, and strengthens the imagination." –
Richelle Goodrich

Richelle's message above captures the essence of transformational daydreaming. I hope you take from this book the tools and techniques you need to create and live a better life—the life that you hope for, desire, and deserve.

The Crossroads

You stand at the crossroads. In folk magic, the crossroads are viewed as a place of power—the place where you make a choice. Choosing is important. As the singer, Gloria Estefan sang a long time ago, *"We seal our fate by the choices we make."*

Now that you've completed this workbook and are becoming ever-more competent in communicating with your subconscious mind, please remember that the choices you make about how to use your new skills are entirely up to you. My only advice is to use them lovingly, wisely, and with honor and integrity.

Thank you for your interest. I wish you much success and happiness as you *daydream your way to a better life!*

Timothy A. Storlie, PhD

List of Main Points for Preview and Review

- ✓ Transformational daydreaming is a special way of using the power of your imagination.

- ✓ When you want to communicate with the subconscious mind, you use contemplation, and that when the subconscious mind wants to communicate with you, it uses spontaneous daydreams.

- ✓ Alpha brainwaves are associated with daydreaming, hypnotic states, and various mystical, paranormal, psychic, spiritual, and transpersonal phenomena.

- ✓ You can use the transformational daydreaming process to explore the realms of the paranormal, enhance your psychic perception, cultivate spiritual values, and experience the transpersonal. All these options and others, may be available to you if you desire, hope, intend, study, learn, practice, explore, and experiment over time.

- ✓ Contemplation can lead to unexpected experiences of insight and expansion of awareness.

- ✓ If you're interested in metaphysical, paranormal, psychic, spiritual, and/or transpersonal matters, you can use the transformational daydreaming process to help imagine, explore, learn, enhance, experiment, and possibly experience. Just ask the magic question, "how could use transformational daydreaming to _____?"

- ✓ The exercise on developing intuition, provides an example of a general process you could use to begin to experience, explore, and experiment with any topic of interest and importance to you.

References

Krippner, S., Bogzaran, F., & De C arvalho, A.P., (2002). *Extraordinary dreams and how to work with them.* Albany, NY: State University of New York Press.

Mish, F.C. (Ed) (2009). *Meriiam-Webster's collegiate dictionary.* Springfiled, MS: Merriam-Webster, Inc.

Master List of All Chapter Main Points for Preview and Review

Chapter 1

- ✓ This is a workbook about hope—the practical hope of creating a better life. How? By learning to communicate with your subconscious mind using the tools of contemplation and daydreaming.

- ✓ Hope is the optimistic belief that people and circumstances can improve—that life can get better. The force of hope is helpful. But—when change is wanted, needed, or required—is it enough? I don't believe so. Truth is, if you hope to *feel* different—if you hope that life will somehow *be* different—then, you must *do* something different. In between hoping and having, some *doing* is required.

- ✓ To make things better, hope has to be practical. It has to have a form (or methods) for nudging a desired possibility toward a greater probability—for transforming the theoretical into the actual.

- ✓ This *doing* requires some type of form for the force to work through. The formula is simple—hoping + doing = having.

- ✓ This book presents a practical, 7-step program on how to communicate and receive advice from the subconscious mind. Using contemplation and daydreaming, you can seek advice on how to experience greater personal, professional, and spiritual growth and development.

- ✓ Frequent repetition of important information is a basic tool of accelerated learning. Repetition is used throughout this book to help quicken your learning, deepen your understanding, and increase your retention.

✓ To accelerate your learning, increase comprehension and retention, and get the most from this book, begin each chapter by first turning to the end of the chapter so you can *preview* the list of main points. After completing your preview, then carefully *read* the chapter and complete each exercise. As you study each chapter, read with the key question in mind. Finally, *review* what you learned by re-reading the list of main points. Also, for your easy preview, review, and reference, you'll find a master list of the collective main points from each chapter located at the back of this book.

✓ Research has consistently demonstrated the benefits of using mental imagery for helping to reduce pain, promote health and wellness, accelerate learning, and enhance performance in the arts and in sports.

✓ The process of daydreaming mobilizes many of the same areas of the brain that would be used if you were physically engaged in these activities. This underscores the effectiveness of using daydreams to practice and rehearse various activities before physically doing them.

✓ For your easy preview, review, and reference, you'll find a master list of the main points from each chapter at the back of this book.

Chapter 2

✓ To accelerate your learning, increase comprehension and retention, and get the most from this book, begin each chapter by first turning to the end of the chapter so you can *preview* the list of main points. After completing your preview, then carefully *read* the chapter and complete each exercise. As you study each chapter, read with the key question in mind. Finally, *review* what you learned by re-reading the list of main points. Also, for your easy preview, review, and reference, you'll find a master list of the collective main points from each chapter located at the back of this book.

- ✓ This chapter introduced you to the subconscious mind — the super intelligence within you — that is at least one million times more powerful than the conscious mind.

- ✓ This super intelligence directs your memory, intuition, dreaming, and daydreaming; never sleeps; governs your body; and is always on duty monitoring, maintaining, regulating, repairing, and healing your body's 37 trillion cells — each cell composed of 100 trillion atoms.

- ✓ The subconscious mind seems willing to communicate with the conscious mind. This two-way communication is the core technique.

- ✓ Your objective is to learn to communicate with the superintelligence within you to seek insight, understanding, creativity, and guidance that can be used to improve your personal and professional life.

- ✓ Responses from the subconscious mind may come as thoughts, memories, images, symbols, sounds, silence, feelings, sensations, dreams, daydreams, and/or any combination of these experiences and others.

- ✓ Holding a view that frames friendship between conscious mind and subconscious mind as healthy and normal, helps it to be healthy and normal. The intentional framing of your relationship with the subconscious mind as friendship with an incredibly wise elder and inner advisor, will help bring this friendship into actuality.

- ✓ The thoughts, feelings, and interpretations you give to friendship with your subconscious mind, can trigger over 1,400 reactions from chemicals, hormones, and neurotransmitters. What you imagine, believe, think, and say, matters.

- ✓ The benefits of framing your relationship with the conscious mind in terms of friendship, allows you to do what you already know how to do, make friends.

- ✓ In exercise #1, the objective was to befriend and name the subconscious mind. The point of naming the subconscious mind is simply to make it easier to hold conversations.

Chapter 3

- ✓ To accelerate your learning, increase comprehension and retention, and get the most from this book, begin each chapter by first turning to the end of the chapter so you can *preview* the list of main points. After completing your preview, then carefully *read* the chapter and complete each exercise. As you study each chapter, read with the key question in mind. Finally, *review* what you learned by re-reading the list of main points. Also, for your easy preview, review, and reference, you'll find a master list of the collective main points from each chapter located at the back of this book.

- ✓ Communicating with the subconscious mind is a skill.

- ✓ Write down the reasons you want to learn transformational daydreaming. This can enhance motivation and quicken learning. Save this list and review it from time to time.

- ✓ Begin a disciplined course of study. Wishing is not enough. True learning requires desiring and *doing*.

- ✓ For most people, *doing* is the most challenging part of the learning process. *Doing* requires persistence and self-discipline.

- ✓ Practice is the key. Your practice should be grounded in the principles of deep, deliberate, accurate practice, and informed by an understanding of the role of repetition, neural pathways, and myelin.

- ✓ Avoidance in trying something new because of a fear of failure is viewed as a psychological defense mechanism designed to help protect you from the emotional pain of possible failure.

- ✓ Remind yourself that skill development, conscious communication with the subconscious mind, expansion of awareness, and the potential of expertise are often experienced just on the other side of fear and excuses.

- ✓ Invest the time and effort required to complete all the exercises.

- ✓ Expect to experience noticeable improvement in your ability to relax and enter an altered state of awareness, to increase contemplation skills, use of multi-sensory imagery, and to increase your ability to befriend and communicate with the subconscious mind.

- ✓ Your learning of transformational daydreaming will unfold through four stages as you move from beginner toward the level of mastery. These four stages are unconscious incompetence, conscious incompetence, conscious competence, and unconscious competence.

- ✓ In your study and practice of transformational daydreaming, you want to achieve *conscious competence* (at the minimum) and hopefully, *unconscious competence.*

- ✓ You will always be a learner. Once you develop expertise, you can develop a little more, then a little more, then a little more after that.

- ✓ Purposefully cultivate a point of view that supports your respectful friendship and working relationship with the subconscious mind.

- ✓ Cultivate a view that embraces the underlying principles of transformational daydreaming, especially the important concepts of contemplation, altered states of awareness, and the role and power of your subconscious mind.

- ✓ There are over 1,400 chemical reactions and over 30 hormones and neurotransmitters that can shift in response to your mental interpretations.

- ✓ Your interpretation matters!

Chapter 4

- ✓ To accelerate your learning, increase comprehension and retention, and get the most from this book, begin each chapter by first turning to the end of the chapter so you can *preview* the list of main points. After completing your preview, then carefully *read* the chapter and complete each exercise. As you study each chapter, read with the key question in mind. Finally, *review* what you learned by re-reading the list of main points. Also, for your easy preview, review, and reference, you'll find a master list of the collective main points from each chapter located at the back of this book.

- ✓ Daydreaming is commonly viewed by most as normal, healthy, and natural.

- ✓ As far as anyone knows, everyone daydreams.

- ✓ Daydreaming is probably the brain's automatic or default activity when attention to the external world is reduced.

- ✓ Daydreaming occurs about every 90 minutes, much like the cycle of nighttime dreaming.

- ✓ Most daydreams are relatively short, averaging from a few seconds to a couple of minutes.

- ✓ Most people's daydreams reflect their preoccupation with current concerns, desires, fantasies, feelings, hopes, goals, and worries.

- ✓ Other popular terms for daydreaming include mind-wandering or waking fantasy.

- ✓ There are two types of daydreaming: intentional and spontaneous daydreaming.

- ✓ It's important to identify your daydreaming patterns and trigger.

- ✓ The core technique of this system is the two-way communication between the conscious mind and the subconscious mind. You use this system to seek insight, information, understanding, creativity, and guidance from the super intelligence within to improve your personal and professional life. It's as if you're asking the subconscious mind for help. The method you are using to ask for help is contemplation. Your subconscious mind—the super intelligence within you—is able and willing to communicate with you. The method the subconscious mind uses to respond to you is through the use of memories, thoughts, feelings, images, symbols, sensations, and sounds—daydreaming.

✓ Consider keeping a daydreaming journal.

Chapter 5

✓ Begin each chapter by first turning to the end of the chapter so you can *preview* the list of main points. After completing your preview, then carefully *read* the chapter and complete each exercise. Finally, *review* what you learned by re-reading the list of main points. Also, for your easy preview, review, and reference, you'll find a master list of the collective main points from each chapter located at the back of this book.

✓ From this point in the book forward, the emphasis shifts from learning to develop a theoretical *view*, to the practical work of learning how to *do*. This is the next important step for you in developing *conscious competence* in the Transformational Daydreaming process.

✓ Since you have completed the *theoretical* Part I of this book and are now entering the *practice* phase, your key question needs to reflect this change. The overarching key question for the remainder of this book is, *How can I use transformational daydreaming to help me _____ ?"* From now on, when you have a concern, question, or problem that can benefit from the insights provided by the subconscious mind, you can ask this question and fill in the missing part with whatever your specific concern might be. For example: *how can I use transformational daydreaming to help me improve my physical health and wellness?*

- ✓ In this chapter, you explored step 1 of the 7-step Transformational Daydreaming program.

- ✓ You selected and named your Safe Place—somewhere where you feel safe, comfortable, and relaxed.

- ✓ To visit your Safe Place, all you need do is intend, close your eyes, repeat its name 3 times, and imagine being there feeling safe, comfortable, and relaxed.

- ✓ There are at least three main uses for your Safe Place; you can use your Safe Place to relax whenever you need to; you can use your Safe Place to contemplate and/or explore any of the more than 37 applications of daydreaming described in chapters 10; and you can use your Safe Place to communicate with the Subconscious Mind.

Chapter 6

- ✓ Begin each chapter by first turning to the end of the chapter so you can *preview* the list of main points. After completing your preview, then carefully *read* the chapter and complete each exercise. Finally, *review* what you learned by re-reading the list of main points. Also, for your easy preview, review, and reference, you'll find a master list of the collective main points from each chapter located at the back of this book.

- ✓ From this point in the book forward, the emphasis shifts from learning to develop a theoretical *view*, to the practical work of learning how to *do*. This is the next important step for you in developing *conscious competence* in the Transformational Daydreaming process.

- ✓ Since you have completed the *theoretical* Part I of this book and are now entering the *practice* phase, your key question needs to reflect this change. The overarching key question for the remainder of this book is, *How can I use transformational daydreaming to help me _____ ?"* From now on, when you have a concern, question, or problem that can benefit from the insights provided by the subconscious mind, you can ask this question and fill in the missing part with whatever your specific concern might be. For example: *how can I use transformational daydreaming to help me improve my physical health and wellness?*

- ✓ Whatever issue you face—whether it's physical, emotional, social, financial, mental, personal, professional, religious, psychic, transpersonal, or spiritual—you can use the same empowering question to orient your view and thought process in a solution-focused manner. Using the transformational daydreaming process, the focus is on *doing*. What can you *do* about your concern?
- ✓ In this chapter, you explored step 2 of the 7-step Transformational Daydreaming program.

- ✓ In step two, you learned to enter an altered state of awareness (or trance) using the Countdown to Relaxation Method, self-suggestion, and a special hand position called a *mudra*.

Chapter 7

---

* Practice Copy – How to Contemplate *

- ✓ Select your topic for contemplation. For example, "I want to improve communication with the subconscious mind." Relax, enter an altered state, and go to your Safe Place (steps 1-2).

- ✓ Resting in your Safe Place, begin by loosely focusing attention on your topic for a couple of minutes. Think about your desired final outcome (end-state). What do you want? What does a successful outcome look, sound, and feel like?

- ✓ Use active imagery. Consciously think about it. Mull it over. Mentally look at it from various viewpoints—through your eyes, through the eyes of another. Ponder. Wonder. Let your thoughts percolate on the subject. Explore possible connections between the concept of your topic and other concepts. What does it remind you of?

- ✓ Remember, your contemplation is a message you are sending to the subconscious mind. You are using an image language rather than a word-based language. Focus on making your message clear. Use all the tricks—the "secret language" (multi-sensory imagery), process-imagery, end-state imagery, receptive and active imagery, multiple points of view, forward and backward chaining, self-talk, emotions, real-time, imagining an actual environment—whatever helps to clearly convey your request.

- ✓ In your contemplation, use step-by-step, process-imagery to show how the outcome is being achieved and end-state imagery that depicts a successful outcome. Experience it as if it's actually happening. Make it real. You need to communicate how you feel about whatever it is you are requesting from the subconscious mind. [note: review the example of meal preparation used in *Exercise 3*]

- ✓ Do all this in a relaxed, curious frame of mind.

- ✓ When done, mentally exit your Safe Place, consciously come back to where you are now. Be fully alert. Return to your normal wakeful awareness and open your eyes.

- ✓ Record a brief summary of your contemplative experience focusing on your thoughts and emotions. Assume everything that happened during your contemplation was related to your stated intention or was part of an answer to a question asked. Honor whatever your experience was by paying attention to it and writing it down.

- ✓ Remember, your experience may be different than expected. Some people contemplate primarily visually. Others are more auditory, kinesthetic, or simply seem to have a general sense of things.

- ✓ Experiences differ from person to person and even from session to session. There is no one right way. There is only your way.

- ✓ There is a difference between using contemplation as a stand-alone technique and using it as part of the entire 7-step process.

- ✓ Master contemplation. It's a skill you can use to improve nearly all aspects of your life, for the rest of your life.

Chapter 8

- ✓ In this chapter, you learned the 4 remaining steps of the 7-step transformational daydreaming process. These steps are: (4) Receive a Daydream; (5) Reorient; (6) Exit Your

Safe Place; and (7) Document, Analyze, and Interpret Your Experience.

- ✓ After you study, learn, and practice all 7 steps, you'll be able to explore and experiment with more than 37 different applications for communicating with your super-intelligence within. These and other suggestions are explored in chapter 10.

- ✓ You learned to begin to recognize the shift that takes place when transitioning from contemplation to spontaneous daydreaming.

- ✓ Your progress using the transformational daydreaming process is rarely linear. It's more realistic to expect a zig-zag journey full of unexpected twists and turns. Knowing this ahead of time will help you avoid disappointment or worse still, blaming yourself for "not doing it right." Learn from your experience. Keep trying. There is no failure, only feedback.

- ✓ Initially you may experience virtually no spontaneous daydreams. That's okay, because with practice, you'll most likely begin experiencing the glimpses and hints described. It's possible that one day you may even experience the holy grail of daydream experiences—the full, spontaneous, and lucid daydream.

- ✓ To improve your daydream recall, the most helpful task you can do is to write it down as soon as you finish your session. The physical act of writing it down helps cement it into your memory and demonstrates that you value the information shared.

- ✓ When reflecting and interpreting your daydreams, you will often experience an "aha." You want to pay special attention to the "aha" moments that are new, novel, and surprising—something that takes you beyond what you already knew.

- ✓ When it comes to interpreting the symbolic language of your daydream, you are your own best expert.

- ✓ The real daydream interpretation comes when you begin to apply the daydream in your daily life. Consider or contemplate what (if anything) will change in your life as a result of applying this new information and/or insight. How could you turn this insight into action?

- ✓ Carefully consider any information you receive from your subconscious mind. Respect the advice given but do not delegate responsibility. You are responsible for the decisions and choices you make, and for the actions you take.

- ✓ In chapter 9, complete instructions for using all 7-steps of the transformational daydreaming process is presented.

Chapter 9

- ✓ Your theoretical preparation and practical work is now complete. Here, for the first time, is the entire 7-step process for communicating with your subconscious mind and receiving insights into how you can create a better life.

The Complete Transformational Daydreaming 7-Step Process

Step 1 – Go to your Safe Place

It begins with hope. Similar to the picture of the boy displayed on the first page of this chapter, you stand and face the future with a desire for more information, insight, and inspiration about a specific concern. Full of this hope, desire, and expectancy, sit or lie down, close your eyes, and imagine entering your Safe Place. Using the method you learned in chapter 5, mentally repeat the name of your Safe Place 3 times. With all your senses , imagine being there now. Make your experience as real as possible. Mentally repeat the phrase, *"safe, relaxed, comfortable."* Feel comfortable and confident as your brain automatically begins to produce more alpha brainwaves. After approximately 60-90 seconds, continue with the next step.

Step 2 – Relax and Enter an Altered State

Use the *countdown-to-relaxation method*. For your ease of reference, it's repeated here. Eventually, it would be preferable if you could complete all steps from memory. But don't worry. There's no hurry.

To memorize these guidelines, most people will need to read through these instructions many times and carry out much mindful practice spread out over a dozen or more sessions. Use the accelerated learning techniques from chapter 3 to help speed up the development of your competency.

- Continue to sit or lie comfortably with your eyes gently closed. Focus your relaxed awareness around your heart area and think, *"As I mentally count down from 7 to 1, I relax more deeply and enter an altered state."* Begin the countdown. Notice (or simply imagine) that with each number you count, you begin to feel more safe, relaxed, and calm. Complete one easy breath for each number you count. As you inhale, think the specific number (or imagine seeing it written on a black or white-board. As you exhale, think the word, *"calm."* Practice this step now.

- With your eyes still closed, keep breathing and mentally counting down. After you reach the number 1, pause to recall any relaxing personal memory for about 20-30 seconds (for example, a relaxing memory from a recent vacation, relaxing in mediation, sitting next to a lake). Practice this step now.

- With your eyes still closed, begin to deepen your altered state of awareness by mentally repeating three times, *"I feel safe, relaxed and comfortable ... I feel safe, relaxed, and comfortable ... I feel safe, relaxed, and comfortable."* Practice this step now.

- To further deepen your altered state, place your hands on your lap and touch the tip of each index finger gently to the tip of each thumb.

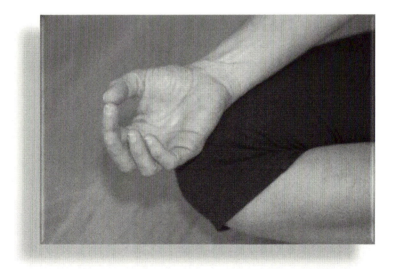

With your eyes still closed, mentally suggest, *"As I count down from 3 to 1, I go deeper into an altered state of awareness. And when I reach the number 1, I'll be in a deeply altered state of awareness."* Without physically moving your head, gently shift your eyes to your right and imagine seeing the number 3 there. With your attention on the right side, slowly and mentally count *"3 ... 3 ... 3."* With your head remaining still, shift your eyes and look to the middle of your visual field — straight out in front of you. With your attention relaxed yet fixed in the middle of your visual field, see the number 2 there. Slowly and mentally count *"2 … 2 … 2."* With your head physically still, shift your eyes gently to the left side of your visual field, see the number 1, and slowly, mentally count *"1 … 1 … 1."* Now rest in a deeply altered state. After 1-2 minutes, continue with step 3. Practice this step now.

Step 3 – Contemplate to Communicate with Subconscious Mind

This is when you ask the subconscious to listen to your concerns. In order for the subconscious mind to respond with a daydream, you first have to connect with it. Using its name — and with your eyes still closed — mentally call out to your subconscious mind. Imagine your subconscious mind — this super power of information and intelligence — is listening. Greet your subconscious mind respectfully and state your purpose. For example, "Hello (name). Thank you for all you do. I would like your help with (your concern). Begin by mentally explaining what you want and why — 2 or 3 sentences is plenty. For example, *"I want to write a book about communicating with my subconscious mind using contemplation and daydreaming. I believe many people will benefit from having access to this information."* That's it. Don't overthink it. After your mental request and explanation, begin to contemplate (communicate) using the multi-sensory imagery process you learned previously in chapter 7.

This is how you "talk" to the subconscious mind. This is how you communicate the details of your concern or question. You do it with your contemplation.

A detailed contemplation provides your subconscious with a multi-sensory impression of your concern. Your contemplation conveys your request and shows the subconscious what you desire.

Contemplate over your request for a few minutes (or for as long as feels right). Combine process imagery to illustrate how your desire might potentially come into being with end-state imagery to showcase the desired outcome—how it looks when it's done or complete. Feel it. Make it as real as possible. Depending on the nature of your request to the subconscious mind, your contemplation could depict a possible beginning, middle, and an end of your desire or concern.

You are contemplating. You hope your subconscious mind will respond with a daydream. This daydream response may come when you've finished your contemplation, not at all, or during your contemplation. You need to be open to timing of your subconscious mind's response.

When the subconscious mind begins to respond, there are many ways you might experience the subtle shift from your directed contemplation to the spontaneous daydream of the subconscious mind. Remember, the subconscious mind could begin to respond while you are still contemplating. If it begins to take over your contemplation and shift to a daydream while you are still contemplating, you need to recognize this is occurring. Carefully read the example below to gain more clarity of how this shift might feel. This can help you learn to recognize when this shift begins so you won't miss it.

Here is one example of how it may feel when this shift from active contemplation to spontaneous daydreaming occurs.

You're sitting with eyes closed in your Safe Place. You feel relaxed and in an altered state. You've asked the subconscious mind for help, and now you're consciously contemplating on your desire. During contemplation, there are moments when your mind seems to wander. You become aware you're not contemplating in the same way you were a moment ago—you're thinking about something completely different. It's as if you catch yourself contemplating upon a different topic. You catch a glimpse of images or maybe the hint of a sound that you didn't purposely choose, and you didn't consciously imagine. These glimpses may or may not be a response from your subconscious mind but pat close attention anyway so that you can recall and document them in the final step 7. Your analysis and interpretation will help you discern if these experiences were a response to your concerns.

As you become more relaxed and drift into a deeper altered state, these momentary lapses often increase. They could even develop into a completely spontaneous daydream. This is a good sign— almost certainly a response from your subconscious mind. Back off your contemplation and allow the subconscious mind full and free reign. If this occurs, your detached observation is a must. Why? Because some people get excited at this point, and guess what? The curtain closes. They lose awareness of the daydream. Why? Too much conscious mind present. This is exactly the point where detached curiosity is critical. Feelings of excitement can shift control away from the subconscious mind back to the conscious mind—just the opposite of what you're trying to do.

Your goal is to receive a response from your subconscious mind in the form of a daydream. Whether your subconscious mind responds *during* your contemplation or *after* you have finished your contemplation, to succeed in this approach, it is critical that you follow the guidelines explained in step 4 below.

Step 4 – Receive a Daydream from Your Subconscious Mind

Stop contemplating. Patiently, passively, and receptively sit, wait, and pay attention. Watch. Listen. Wait for the subconscious to respond. Sit with a curious attitude of detached expectancy and remain open to what might happen, no matter how mundane or surprising.

Allow the subconscious mind complete freedom and autonomy to direct the daydreaming process with no conscious interference from you. This communication process has virtually no chance of succeeding unless you're willing to take your hands off the steering wheel, allow the subconscious mind to show up when it's good and ready, take its place in the driver's seat, and drive the bus free of your judgment and micro-management. [FYI - this is easier said than done.]

Allow any daydreaming activity to unfold spontaneously. Be receptive to what occurs. Remember, the response from your subconscious mind can range from nothing at all: to a glimpse of faint and confusing images; a mixed grab bag of personal memories; barely audible words or sounds; subtle impressions, sensations, or feelings; and any and all possible combinations of these experiences; all the way to the experience of a full mental movie. When step 4 feels complete, you've had enough, or nothing has occurred within a reasonable amount of time, you can begin to close the daydreaming process.

Many people require several attempts before noticing any subconscious response. If no recognizable response is forthcoming within 10-20 minutes,

- Thank the subconscious mind for listening.
- Ask the subconscious mind for its help in recognizing its response when it does come.
- Follow the steps to conclude your session.
- Try another day and trust that every step you take, takes you a step closer to success.

Step 5 – Return to Normal, Wakeful Awareness

When the daydream feels complete or you have decided to conclude your session for other reasons, what do you do? You thank your subconscious mind and begin the process of returning to your ordinary state of normal, wakeful awareness. Mentally suggest to yourself that in the next few seconds, when you open your eyes, you will feel awake, alert, fully conscious, and with excellent recall of whatever you may have experienced..

Step 6 – Exit Your Safe Place

Before leaving, remind yourself that you can return to your Safe Place anytime you want by simply intending to, closing your eyes, and mentally repeating the name of your Safe Place three times. Then, gently open your eyes, bringing all of your experiences, learnings, insights, and "aha's" with you.

Step 7 – Document, Analyze, and Interpret Your Daydream

Please stop! Do not engage in any other activity until you complete this final step. Why? Because daydreams are like night dreams. Both are easily forgotten and can quickly evaporate in the presence of competing thoughts. After all…

What's the point of completing this 7-step process for communicating with your subconscious mind if afterword you can't recall the advice given?

To improve your daydream recall, the most helpful task you can do is to write your daydream down immediately after you finish your session. The physical act of writing it down helps cement it into your memory.

Write down only what you can specifically recall of your daydream experience. This is not the time for guesswork, speculation, or interpretation. That will come later. Like the dreams of the night, the dreams of the day are symbolic (Barth, 1997). Yet daydream interpretation involves much more than simply translating symbols.

Remember a daydream can range from a glimpse of vague images, feelings, sensations, sounds, smells, and fleeting personal memories, to a full mental movie. What did you experience specifically? As you record your daydream, regard everything you experienced as potentially useful information. Assume all aspects of your daydream were symbolically related to your concern. Write everything you can recall down on paper before proceeding. Just the facts as you recall them. Simply describe your actual experience.

When you have recorded as much as you can honestly recall, then ask yourself if you believe your subconscious responded to your request for help. Did it respond? If your answer is yes, take a moment to celebrate that it really happened. This is an important achievement you can build and expand upon.

If you believe you had a genuine response from the subconscious mind, then the next most important task is to begin the process of daydream interpretation. Ask, "What is this daydream trying to tell me?" (Feinstein & Krippner, 2006).

Reflect on your daydream in its entirety. Try to capture the holistic essence of its message by summarizing what you can recall into a single phrase or sentence—similar to the title of a movie.

Again, ask, "what is this daydream trying to tell me?" What comes to you when you ask this question? How does the daydream make you feel? What does it remind you of?

Did this daydream provide you with any immediate, obvious, fresh insight into your concern? If so, describe this insight with as much detail as you feel is helpful. What was your subconscious trying to tell you? What is the single most important insight this response is trying to communicate to you? You are building toward an interpretation and there could be more than one.

A note of caution, especially if you received a lot of information. When working toward daydream interpretation, favor insights and information that are creative, new, novel, and surprising. Also, when reflecting upon your daydream—in its entirety or in its parts—you will often experience an "aha."

Taylor, (2009) describes the "aha" recognition as a trustworthy guide to discovering authentic, accurate interpretations but cautions that the initial aha moments are likely to occur over things you already know or recognize. The treasure lies in the sense of surprise—the "aha" that takes you beyond what you already know. Delaney (1996) agrees. She writes, "You will know that you have succeeded in interpreting your dream when it tells you something you did not realize before."

After all, why would your subconscious mind waste time communicating something you already think you know? Be cautious of responses that only seem to confirm what you already know, believe, or suspect.

Next, look at the individual parts and symbols of the daydream. List the people, places, activities, images, sounds, sensations, emotions, you observed. What feelings do you have about each of these images? What words or ideas come to mind when you recall this image? Do you feel energized by this image? Does this image remind you of anything that is connected to your concern? Ask yourself, "What is this like? What does this remind me of?"

When it comes to interpreting the symbolic language of your daydream, you are your own best expert. If you believe you had a genuine response experience but the meaning was confusing or seemed unrelated to your request, what is your best guess as to its meaning? Pretend you know. You can always contemplate further upon this using the advanced techniques you learned.

Finally, as Thurston (1978) reminded, the real dream interpretation comes when you begin to discover applications of daydream insights in your daily life. How could you turn insight into action? Consider or contemplate what (if anything) will change in your life as a result of applying this new information and/or insight. In your imagination, implement the response received. How does that feel?

List several ways you might practically act on the response to create a better life (Johnson, 1986). Make a plan for carrying out your choice. Mentally rehearse your plan using the technique of contemplation learned. Consider the advice given, but do not delegate your responsibility. Evaluate the risk and benefits before taking physical action. You are responsible for the decisions you make and the actions you take.

This final step of *Document, Analyze, and Interpret Your Daydream* may seem long, confusing, and cumbersome to you. If so, please don't worry. There's a simple explanation and solution. The explanation can be found in the 4-stage model for developing competency explained in chapter 3.

According to the 4-stage model, since you've just been exposed to a lot of new information, any feelings of confusion you may have are normal. Why? Because at this stage of your learning about how to conduct daydream analysis and interpretation, you are probably operating at the level of *conscious incompetence*. Yes, you are acquiring theoretical knowledge about daydream interpretation, but you have yet to actually do it.

You simply lack the required experience at this point. That is the explanation. The solution follows next.

The solution to any confusion is deep, deliberate practice. If you use the principles of deep practice (as discussed in chapter 3), to further develop your skills of daydream analysis and interpretation, the 4-stage model for developing competency, predicts you will evolve from the second stage of *conscious incompetence* to the third stage of learning—*conscious competence*. And after that, even further. The key is your deep, deliberate practice.

And remember, when faced with a problem or concern, you can always ask the magic question, *"How can I use transformational daydreaming to help me improve my skills of daydream analysis and interpretation?"*

If you understand, respect, and apply the structure and ritual of the overall 7-step process, you'll eventually discover it takes on a life of its own, strengthens your intent, and makes it easier for you to successfully communicate with your subconscious mind. Try it. Test it. Prove it. Your subconscious is willing to communicate with you but are you listening?

Once again, congratulations! You've not only learned the entire 7-step transformational daydreaming process, you've assembled an impressive set of tools that you can begin to use to help create a better personal and/or professional life. This collection of tools and techniques is the main focus of the next chapter.

If you understand, respect, and apply the structure and ritual of the overall 7-step process, you'll eventually discover it takes on a life of its own, strengthens your intent, and makes it easier for you to successfully communicate with your subconscious mind. Try it. Test it. Prove it. Your subconscious is willing to communicate with you but are you listening?

Chapter 10

- ✓ You now have an impressive set of tools you can use to help improve nearly every aspect of your life—personal, professional, physical, emotional, mental, social, sexual, financial, creative, philosophical, metaphysical, mystical, psychic, transpersonal, and spiritual.

- ✓ This chapter lists 22 tools and techniques that were presented (see the *Master List of Chapter Main Points* located at the end of this book).

- ✓ 37 areas that you can explore, experiment, and experience are listed under the categories of physical, emotional and relationships, intellectual and mental, business and professional, and imaginal conversations.

- ✓ The questions you ask, determine the answers you get. Want a higher quality answer? Ask a higher quality question?

- ✓ For the rest of your life, you can use your skills to improve the quality of nearly every aspect of your life.

Chapter 11

- ✓ Transformational daydreaming is a special way of using the power of your imagination.

- ✓ When you want to communicate with the subconscious mind, you use contemplation, and that when the subconscious mind wants to communicate with you, it uses spontaneous daydreams.

- ✓ Alpha brainwaves are associated with daydreaming, hypnotic states, and various mystical, paranormal, psychic, spiritual, and transpersonal phenomena. You can use the transformational daydreaming process to explore the realms of the paranormal, enhance your psychic perception, cultivate spiritual values, and experience the transpersonal. All these options and others, may be available to you if you desire, hope, intend, study, learn, practice, explore, and experiment over time.

- ✓ Contemplation can lead to unexpected experiences of insight and expansion of awareness.

- ✓ If you're interested in metaphysical, paranormal, psychic, spiritual, and/or transpersonal matters, you can use the transformational daydreaming process to help imagine, explore, learn, enhance, experiment, and possibly experience. Just ask the magic question, "how could use transformational daydreaming to _____?"

- ✓ The exercise on developing intuition, provides an example of a general process you could use to begin to experience, explore, and experiment with any topic of interest and importance to you.

References

Achterberg, J., & Dossey, B., Kolkmeier, L. (1994). *Rituals of healing: Using imagery for health and wellness.* New York: NY: Bantam Books.

Barth, D. (1997). *Unlock the creative power of daydreams.* NY, NY: Penguin Group.

Baruss, I. (2003). *Alterations of consciousness: An empirical analysis for social scientists.* Washington, D.C.: American Psychological Association.

Bone, P.F., & Ellen, P.S. (1992). The generation and consequences of communication-evoked imagery. *Journal of Consumer Research, 19,* 93-104.

Bosnak, R. (1988). *A little course in dreams.* Boston, MS: Shambhala.

Bristow, W. (2004). *The art of the daydream.* London, UK: MQ Pub.

Coyle, D. (2009). *The talent code.* New York, NY: Bantam Books.

Delaney, G. (1996). *Living your dreams.* NY, NY: HarperCollins.

Dawson, C. (2007). *The genie in your genes.* Santa Rosa, CA: Elite Books.

Feinstein, D., & Krippner, S. (2006). *The mythic path.* Santa Rosa, CA: Energy Psychology Press.

Freeman, L.W., & Lawlis, G.F. (2001). *Mosby's complementary and alternative medicine: A research-based approach.* St. Louis, MO: Mosby.

Fries, A. (2009). *Daydreams at work: Wake up your creative powers.* Sterling, VA: Capital Books.

Gale Reference Team. (2001). Daydreaming. *Gale Encyclopedia of Psychology.*

Glausiusz, J. (2014). *Living in an imaginary world.* https://www.scientificamerican.com/article/living-in-an-imaginary-world/

Johnson, R. (1986). *Inner work using dreams and active imagination for personal growth.* NY, NY: Harper One.

Kabat-Zinn (1990). *Full catastrophe living: Using the wisdom of your body and mind to face stress, pain, and illness.* New York, NY: Bantam Dell.

Klinger, E. (1990). *Daydreaming: Using waking fantasy and imagery for self-knowledge and creativity.* Los Angeles: Tarcher.

Krippner, S., Bogzaran, F., & De C arvalho, A.P., (2002). *Extraordinary dreams and how to work with them.* Albany, NY: State University of New York Press.

Lahey, J. (2013). Teaching kids to daydream. https://www.theatlantic.com/education/archive/2013/10/teach-kids-to-daydream/280615/

Lehrer, J. (2012). *The virtues of daydreaming.* http://www.newyorker.com/tech/frontal cortex/the-virtues-of-daydreaming.

Mish, F.C. (Ed) (2009). *Meriiam-Webster's collegiate dictionary.* Springfiled, MS: Merriam-Webster, Inc.

Morris, T., Spittle, M., and Watt, A. (2005). *Imagery in sport.* Champaign, ILL: Human Kinetics.

Murphy, S. (2005). *The sport psychology handbook.* Champaign, IL: Human Kinetics.

Rao, R.K. (2002). *Consciousness Studies: Cross-cultural perspectives.* Jefferson, NC: McFarland & Co.

Rossman, M. (2000). *Guided imagery for self-healing.* Novato, CA: New World Library.

Sheikh, A.A., & Shelkh, K.S. (eds) (1989). *Eastern & Western approaches to healing: Ancient wisdom and modern knowledge.* New York, NY: Wiley.

Siddle, B.K. (2008). *Sharpening the warrior's edge: The psychology of science and training.* Belleville, IL: PPCT Research Publications.

Singer, J. (1975). *The inner world of daydreaming.* New York, NY: Harper & Row.

Singer, J. (2009). Researching imaginative play and adult consciousness: Implications for daily and literary creativity. Psychology of Aesthetics, Creativity, and the Arts 3(4), 190-199.

Smallwood, J., Beach, E., Schooler, J.W., & Handy, T.C. (2008). Going AWOL in the brain: Mind wandering reduces cortical analysis of external events. Journal of Cognitive Neuroscience 20(3), 4.

Storlie, T. (2015). *Person-centered communication with older adults.* San Diego, CA: Academic Press.

Taylor, J. (2009). *The wisdom of your dreams.* NY, NY: The Penguin Group.

Thurston, M. (1978). *How to interpret your dreams.* Virginia Beach, VA: A.R.E. Press.

Whitmore, P.G. (2009). A new mindset for a new mind: understanding new theories about how the brain works, and what it can mean for adult learning. *American Society for Training and Development. T + D,* 60-65, http://www.astd.org.

Timothy A. Storlie, PhD

ABOUT THE AUTHOR

Timothy A. Storlie, Ph.D., is a daydreamer and a passionate advocate for lifelong learning. As a psychologist, instructor, licensed counselor, medical social worker, hypnotherapist, adult educator, researcher and writer, the common thread connecting all services is his passion for learning and teaching.

Dr. Storlie's professional interests include health and wellness, the study of consciousness, transpersonal psychology, cross-cultural spirituality, adult education, critical thinking and reasoning, hypnosis, meditation, and sports performance enhancement. Timothy graduated from historic Saybrook University where he earned a Ph.D. in Psychology with a dual concentration in *Integrative Health Studies* and *Consciousness and Spirituality*. He also completed a post-doctoral certificate in *Dream Studies*. Timothy earned his B.S. in Education from Portland State University and two graduate degrees also from PSU—an M.S. in Special Education and an MSW in Social Work.

Author of several books, articles, and publications, Dr. Storlie's most recent book is *Person-Centered Communication with Older Adults: The Professional Providers Guide*. He maintains a private counseling practice and can be contacted through his website at www.associatedcounselors.org

May I ask a favor?

I hope you found this book helpful. If you did, would you please post an online review? I'd really appreciate it! Your constructive comments are helpful to me and to other potential readers. It's easy and only takes a couple of minutes. Here's how you do it.

1. Go to www.Amazon.com
2. Type in *Transformational Daydreaming*
3. Click on my book
4. Scroll down and click on *Write a Customer Review*

Thank you for your comments!

Timothy A. Storlie, PhD

Made in the USA
Las Vegas, NV
16 July 2021